Days Out
IN AND AROUND
LONDON

Days Out
IN AND AROUND
LONDON

Pauline Gorman

Longman

Acknowledgements

It is not everyone researching a book such as this who has the good fortune to have a colleague with a filing cabinet full of information gathered over several years. Shirley Godleman has given me access to those files and has also updated them and encouraged me since. Wendy Camm, Vivienne Evans, Vera Williams and Hilary Stuckey supplied more information and Jo Williams, Daniel Walsh and my son Rickard helped me to put the details together. Jean Taggart and Eric and Hilda Double handled a great number of telephone messages.

My thanks to all the above-mentioned for their help and also to the many owners, directors, curators and educational liaison officers who patiently supplied all the information for this book.

LONGMAN GROUP LIMITED
Longman House
Burnt Mill, Harlow, Essex CM20 2JE, England
and associated companies throughout the world

© Longman Group Limited 1986

First published 1986
ISBN 0 582 23540 5

Set in Times New Roman

Produced by Longman Group (FE) Ltd
Printed in Hong Kong

Introduction

This book is a guide to places of educational interest, in the broadest sense, in and within a 25 miles radius of London. It is written for parents, teachers and tourists – anyone who plans a trip with children. It is full of practical as well as other detailed information, in the hope that this will ensure trips are enjoyed as much as possible.

My research brought me into contact with those who own or oversee the various establishments. I was impressed by their enthusiasm for the many projects they undertake and the care with which they present their exhibits for the public. In spite of some fears that vital grants will be withdrawn, they are optimistic and plan ahead to meet the needs of changing public interest and awareness.

Some places provide introductory leaflets which state, in friendly and direct terms, their aims and hopes. Some are expanding their educational facilities by the provision of worksheets, talks and tours aimed at specific age-groups and areas of interest. Many will integrate school work with lectures, videos, etc. and organise 'handling' sessions. All these features will encourage children to think of these places as friendly and interesting ones, which they will want to visit again.

Every establishment is conscious of the need to make access available for the disabled. Where buildings are unsuitable for modification (having to be preserved in their original state), there is genuine regret that this is not possible.

ABBEY MILLS PUMPING STATION

(See Thames Water Sewage Treatment Works and Pumping Stations.)

ALL HALLOWS BY THE TOWER

Byward Street, London EC3R 5BJ
Tel: 01-481 2928

Underground: Tower Hill

Open
9 a.m. – 5.45 p.m. Mon to Fri;
10 a.m. – 5.45 p.m. Sat and Sun.
Closed 26, 27 and 28 Dec.

Admission charges
Free
Entrance to Museum 75p

All Hallows by the Tower has stood for over 1300 years and survived the Great Fire and World War bombs. The original Saxon arch (dated around the second half of the 7th century) has Roman tiles, and the Undercroft Museum has a perfect tessellated Roman pavement.

The Museum also has Roman artefacts, including lamps, tiles and nails and a display of church plate. The church registers survive from the 16th century and record all aspects of human life – baptism, marriage and burial.

Brass rubbing can be done – charges, which include materials and instruction, from 50p to £3.50.

Special events
On May 16, Ascension Day, the ceremony of the Beating of the Bounds takes place at 3 p.m. This is when boys from St Dunstans take a boat on the river and one boy is dangled by his ankles over the side at each boundary. The boys then walk round the shoreside boundaries, beating the marker points with long canes.

3

Educational provision
Worksheets are in preparation.

Refreshments
Church refectory open 12 a.m. – 3 p.m. Mon to Fri.

Shop
Bookstall open 11 a.m. – 5 p.m.; sells books and souvenirs.

APSLEY HOUSE

149 Piccadilly, London W1V 9FA
Tel: 01-499 5676

Underground: Hyde Park Corner

Open
10 a.m. – 6 p.m. Tues to Thurs and Sat; 2.30 – 6 p.m. Sun.
Closed Mon and Fri and Good Friday, May Day, Christmas
Eve, Christmas Day, Boxing Day and New Year's Day.

Admission charges
Children 30p.
Adults 60p.
School Parties free.

Apsley House was the home of the first Duke of Wellington,
was designed by Robert Adam and built in 1771-78. In 1818
Benjamin Dean Wyatt was employed to alter the house and in
1828 to 1830 he added the Waterloo Gallery. The House
contains many Wellington relics including porcelain from
Sevres, Berlin and Meissen and paintings by Velasquez,
Van Dyke, Correggio, Murillo and Goya. It offers superb
opportunities for viewing and studying this important period
of European History – the early 19th century.

Educational provision
Educational institutions can book a guide-lecturer by
telephoning Andrea Aspy on 01-589 6371 (extension 316).

Shop

A small gift store, open during visiting hours, sells postcards and catalogues.

Disabled

There are some steps to the ground floor, a lift to the first floor and wheelchair access to some parts.

ARSENAL FOOTBALL STADIUM

Avenell Road, Highbury, London N5
Tel: 01-226 0304

Underground: Arsenal

Open

Tours by appointment only at 10.30 a.m., 11 a.m. and 2 p.m. Mon to Fri.
Closed Sat and Sun.

The **Arsenal Football Stadium** has a guided tour taking about 1½ hours. Visitors are taken right round the stadium and can visit the dresing room and boardroom if they are not in use at the time. The tour takes in the JVC training centre, the pitch, the press room, trophies cabinet and the commentary gives a history of the club and details of all the features. Photographs can be taken and autographs collected from players, if present.

Shop

Shop open during tours sells badges, postcards, books, scarves, hats, football kits and souvenirs.

Disabled

This visit is not suitable for the disabled because of the many steps.

AVERY HILL WINTER GARDEN

Bexley Road, Eltham, London SE9
Tel: 01-850 2666

British Rail: Falconwood

Open
1–4 p.m. Mon to Fri; 11 a.m.–4 p.m. Sat and Sun.
Closed first Mon in each month and Christmas Day.

Admission charges
Free.

Avery Hill Winter Garden has tropical and sub-tropical plants
including trees from India, plants from South America,
flowers from Africa and lemon, pineapple and banana trees.
There are many more exotic plants and ornamental pools,
fountains, and a marble statue of the Greek goddess Galatea.

Disabled
Wheelchair access to the Garden.

BADEN-POWELL HOUSE

Queen's Gate, London SW7 5JS
Tel: 01-584 7030

Underground: Gloucester Road

Open
9 a.m.–7 p.m. Daily.
Never closed.

Admission charges
Free.

Baden-Powell House is the HQ of the Scout Movement in this country. At the house there is a small exhibition tracing the life of Lord Robert Baden-Powell, founder of the scout movement, and the only Chief Scout of the World there has ever been.

There are photographs of Baden-Powell's life from his military career as well as his scouting expeditions, a replica of the first scout camp formed at Brown Sea Island, Poole Harbour, Dorset in 1907, and tapes of Baden-Powell's last messages.

The exhibition is not large; it takes about 30 minutes to view and could be visited in conjunction with other larger museums situated nearby.

Educational provision
A free visitors' guide and house quiz are available.

Refreshments
Cafeteria open for main meal.

Shop
Shop open during visiting hours selling scouting souvenirs.

Disabled
There is a ramp up the entrance steps, and the main part of the museum is on the ground floor. A lift goes up to the higher floors and toilet facilities are available.

BAKELITE MUSEUM

12 Mundania Court, Forest Hill Road, East Dulwich, London SE23
Tel: 01-961 2240

British Rail: Honor Oak

Open

By appointment only. The Bakelite Museum Society is seeking larger and more appropriate premises to house a 'National Plastics Museum'.

Admission charges

Free to members and friends of the Bakelite Museum Society.

The **Bakelite Museum** has a unique collection of plastics from the beginning of its development in the mid-19th century, with specimens such as Parkesine, Vulcanite and Shellac, with a concise collection of Bakelite and Urea Formaldehyde. Some 250 radios are included in the collection. Early plastic domestic ware, kitchenware and decorative items are on display. Slide packages and a short lecture on the 'History of Plastics' are available. Gadgets, machinery and mechanisms can be demonstrated.

Educational provision

Whilst sponsorship is being sought there are only very minimum provisions and the Museum is confined to members only, limited numbers of students and parties not exceeding 8 persons.

Refreshments

Refreshments available in Melamine, Bakelite or Tupperware cups.

BANKSIDE GALLERY

48 Hopton Street, Blackfriars, London SE1 9JH
Tel: 01-928 7521

Underground: Blackfriars and London Bridge
British Rail: London Bridge

Open
10 a.m. – 5 p.m. Tues to Sat; 2 – 6 p.m. Sun.
Closed Mon.

Admission charges
Children   25p.
Adults   50p.

The **Bankside Gallery** is the home of the Royal Society of Painters in Watercolours and the Royal Society of Painter-Etchers and Engravers. Each Society holds a Spring and Autumn exhibition. The spacious and elegant gallery also presents important contemporary and historical exhibitions from Britain and abroad, which reflect its forward-looking educational role. Its aim is to make accessible to artists, the general public and gallery-goers, the heritage and potential of the arts of painting, drawing and printing on paper.

Shop
Kiosk open in the gallery, selling books and postcards.

BANQUETING HOUSE

Whitehall, London SW1
Tel: 01-930 4179

Underground: Embankment or Westminster
British Rail: Charing Cross

Open

10 a.m. – 5 p.m. Tues to Sat; 2 – 5 p.m. Sun.
Closed on Mon, Christmas Eve, Christmas Day, Boxing Day,
New Year's Day, Good Friday and at short notice for
government functions.

Admission charges

Children (under 16) 25p
Adults 50p.
O.A.P. 25p.
School Parties
Free on prior application.

The **Banqueting House** was built in 1619-22 to the design of
Inigo Jones as part of the great Palace of Whitehall which from
1530 to 1698 was the sovereign's metropolitan residence. The
magnificent painted ceiling by Rubens was commissioned by
Charles I and installed in 1634-5. He passed the painting on the
way to his execution, which took place on a scaffold set up just
in front of the present entrance. It was the scene, too, for the
restoration of his son and the formal offer of the throne to
William and Mary after the flight of James II in 1688.

Architecturally, the building helped to set the style for large
public and private building until well into the 19th century.
The interior has recently been restored as nearly as possible to
its original appearance with a copy of a Stuart throne set up at
the south end.

Educational provision

A general education sheet is available free for teachers.

Shop

Shop open during visiting hours sells guidebooks, colour
postcards, slides and souvenirs.

BARBICAN CENTRE TOUR

Silk Street, London EC2Y 8DS
Tel: 01-638 4141 extension 218

Underground: Barbican (closed Sun), Moorgate and
Liverpool Street

Open
9 a.m. – 11 p.m. Mon to Sat; 12 noon – 11 p.m. Sun; Tours start
12.25 p.m. and 5.15 p.m. Mon to Sat. Pre-booking for the tour
is advisable.
Closed Christmas Eve and Christmas Day.

Admission charges
Children   £1 (no brochure).
Adults   £2 (including brochure).
OAP, Student, Disabled   £1 (no brochure).
Parties of 10 or more   £1.50 per person (no brochure).

The **Barbican Centre Tour** varies according to accessibility
and normally takes in the main auditoria (the Concert Hall and
the Theatre), the Cinema and the main Foyers, continuing to
the upper levels of the Centre. The History and development
of the Centre and current procedures are explained and
questions willingly answered. There are usually free
exhibitions in the foyers.

Art Gallery exhibitions (for which an entrance charge is
payable)
For details of exhibitions, phone the Barbican Centre.

Refreshments
Carvery 12 noon – 3 p.m. for lunches, 6 p.m. until half-hour
after end of last performance for dinner.

Disabled
A tour for the disabled is available by arrangement.

BARN ELMS RESERVOIR

(See Thames Water Reservoirs.)

BATTERSEA DOG'S HOME

4 Battersea Park Road, London SW8 4AA
Tel: 01-622 3626

British Rail: Battersea Park and Queenstown Road

Open
9.30 a.m. – 4.30 p.m. Mon to Fri.
Closed on Sat, Sun, Bank holidays.

Admission charges
Children 10p.
Adults 20p.
OAP 10p.

Battersea Dogs' Home dates from 1860 when it was based in
Holloway and then transferred to Battersea. It takes in about
350 stray dogs each week and has about 600 dogs at any one
time. The public can come and visit the home and buy the
dogs and also cats.

Educational provision
A film 'Dog Days' is available free for schools from:
Guild Sound and Vision, Guild House, Oundle Road,
Peterborough, PE2 9PZ.

BATTERSEA PARK CHILDREN'S ZOO

Battersea Park, London SW11
Tel: 01-228 9957

British Rail: Battersea Park

Open
1.30 – 5.30 p.m. Mon to Fri; 11 a.m. – 6 p.m. Sat,
Sun, Bank and School holidays.
Closed during the winter (beginning of October to first
week of Easter).

Admission charges
Free.

Battersea Park Children's Zoo has lemurs, monkeys, fennec
foxes, marmosets, otters, wallabies, cranes, parrots, ibis, sheep
and goats. There is a deer enclosure with axis deer, black buck
and guinea fowl.

Refreshments
Cafeteria open all year round 10 a.m. – 7 p.m. or 8 p.m. or dusk
if earlier.·

Disabled
Wheelchair access is good.

BATTERSEA PUPPET CENTRE

(See Puppets Centre.)

BATTLE OF BRITAIN MUSEUM

Grahame Park Way, Hendon, London NW9 5LL
(same site as RAF and Bomber Command Museums)
Tel: 01-205 2266

Underground: Colindale

Open
10 a.m. – 6 p.m. Mon to Sat; 2 – 6 p.m. Sun.
Closed Christmas Eve, Christmas Day, Boxing Day,
New Year's Day, Good Friday and May Day.

Admission charges
Children   50p.
Adults   £1.
OAP   50p.
Groups of 20 and above
Children   25p.
Adults   75p.

The **Battle of Britain Museum** is adjacent to the RAF Museum
and is the only national memorial to the men, women and
machines, involved in the decisive Air Battle of 1940. The
aircraft are displayed along the sides of the building with the
RAF aircraft facing their erstwhile adversaries. The Spitfire
and Hurricane are shown in an imaginative replica of a
camouflaged dispersal pen of the type used on Fighter
Command stations in 1940. Other RAF aircraft on display
include the Gladiator, Blenheim IV and only surviving
Defiant. Luftwaffe machines include the Heinkel III, JU88,
ME110, JU87G and the Stuka Dive-bomber. The Museum's
galleries contain references to supporting organisations
including the Royal Observer Corps, anti-aircraft defences,
radar and balloons. The central feature is a replica of an
operations room.

Educational provision
Sample worksheets for children of both primary and
secondary age, for duplication, may be obtained from the
Education Officer. Short introductory slide talks can be given
by prior arrangement with the Education Officer, on weekdays
only between 10 a.m. – 12.30 p.m.

Refreshments
Self-service cafeteria open 10 a.m. – 5 p.m. Mon to Sat and
2 – 5 p.m. on Sun. Children's menu on application. Picnic
building seats 50.

Shop
Opens with the Museum and closes one hour earlier, sells postcards, posters, aviation books, plastic kits, slides and souvenirs.

Disabled
All parts of the museum are accessible by wheelchair.

BAYHURST WOOD COUNTRY PARK

Breakspear Road North, Harefield, Middlesex
Tel: (Uxbridge) 0895 50111

Underground: Ruislip

Open
7.30 a.m. to dusk Daily.
Never closed.

Admission charges
Free.

Bayhurst Wood Country Park is 100 acres of ancient broadleaf woodland with nature trail and bridle path. An open air museum of woodland crafts is under construction and the charcoal burner encampment is completed. Demonstrations of woodland crafts and guided walks can be arranged with the Warden Mr G Mist (tel: (Ruislip) 089 56 30078). There are picnic areas and barbeque facilities are bookable. Note, there are no shelters in the park so visits on rainy days are not advised.

Refreshments
Refreshment bar open from May to September.

Disabled
There are special toilet and picnic facilities for the disabled.

BEAR GARDENS MUSEUM

1 Bear Gardens, Bankside, Southwark, London SE1 9EB
Tel: 01-928 6342

Underground: Mansion House and London Bridge
British Rail: London Bridge and Waterloo

Open
10 a.m. – 5.30 p.m. Tues to Sat; 2 – 6 p.m. Sun.
Closed Mon, Christmas Eve, Christmas Day, Boxing Day and
New Year's Day.

Admission charges
Children   50p.
Adults   £1.
OAP, UB40 and *local residents*   50p.

The **Bear Gardens Museum** traces the history of the
Shakespearean stage from 1576 to 1642, through a series of text
panels and illustrations. There are several models of the
outdoor and indoor playhouses, including one of the
Globe Theatre Complex which the international Shakespeare
Globe Centre is planning to re-build on Bankside. There is
also a replica of the '1616' Cockpit Stage, Drury Lane.

Lecture tours of the museum are given to groups at a flat rate
of £15 plus admission. Additional lectures or workshops on
specific texts cost £30 and take place on the '1616' Cockpit
Stage.

Educational provision
Worksheets are being produced, and there will be animated
lectures, with 'live' performances, available in 1985.

Refreshments
There are facilities to sell coffee to groups on lecture tours.

Shop
Shop open during visiting hours sells books on various aspects
of the theatre of the 16th and 17th centuries, including texts of
plays, postcards, Wedgewood china related to Shakespeare
and antique prints.

Disabled
The museum is on the ground-floor level except for the '1616' stage which is housed upstairs.

BEDDINGTON SEWAGE FARM

(See Thames Water Sewage Treatment Works and Pumping Stations.)

BEDFORDS PARK NATURE TRAIL

Bedfords Park, Romford. Essex
(Entrance from Lower Bedfords Road, or from the car park entered from Broxhill Road)
Tel: (Romford) 0708 66999 extension 253

British Rail: Harold Wood or Romford

Open:
8 a.m. – half an hour after sunset (between 4.30 and 9.30 p.m.) Daily.
Never closed.

Admission charges
Free.

Bedfords Park Nature Trail has recently been refurbished and now has three different length routes taking from 3/4 of an hour to 1 1/2 hours. All the routes begin past the cafeteria and the large Californian sequoia – redwood tree. The longer route also passes a monkey-puzzle tree and a Lebanese cedar. The red deer in the deer pens have been established in a herd from four deer introduced in the 1940s. Depending, of course on the time of year, many butterflies, birds, flowers and insects can be seen. As the estate has been used for recreational purposes for many years, the vegetation is not typical of surrounding areas, which are heathland. However, the undulating slopes provide a delightful sequence of ever-changing vistas across the dry grassy slopes down into the Larch Wood valley, through lush meadows to the lake, finally returning to the hilltop by the deer pens, among the planted parkland of the old estate.

Educational provision
A trail guide is available from the cafeteria when open and from local libraries.

Refreshments
Cafeteria open in the summer.

BEKONSCOT MODEL VILLAGE

Bekonscot, Beaconsfield, Bucks HP9 2PZ
Tel: 049-46 2919

British Rail: Beaconsfield

Open
Mar 1 – Oct 31 10 a.m. – 5 p.m. Daily.
Closed Nov to Feb.

Admission charges
Children 50p.
Adults £1.
OAP, Students and *UB40* 70p.
School Parties
Children 35p, Adults 70p.
Note: Mondays and Fridays are the best days to visit.

Bekonscot is the oldest model village in the world. A wonderland in miniature, comprising castles, churches, houses and shops, through which runs the finest outdoor model railway open to the public in the UK. All this is in a beautiful landscaped garden. Up to six trains run at any one time through the miniature village.

Educational provision
Teachers' notes are available and 12 slides can be sent on free loan plus postage costs.

Refreshments
Refreshment kiosk open 11 a.m. – 2.45 p.m.

Shop
Shop open during visiting hours sells souvenirs.

BELFAST, HMS

**Symons Wharf, Vine Lane, Tooley Street, London SE1 2JH
Tel: 01-407 6434**

Underground: Tower Hill
British Rail: London Bridge

Open
Mar 20 to Oct 31   11 a.m. – 5.30 p.m. (last admission 5.20 p.m.) Daily.
Nov 1 to Mar 19   11 a.m. – 4.30 p.m. (last admission 4 p.m.) Daily.
Closed New Year's Day, Good Friday, first Mon in May, Christmas Eve, Christmas Day, Boxing Day.

Admission charges
Children   £1.
Adults   £2.
Student and UB40   £1.
School Parties
Children   70p.
Adult   £1.40, (one free adult for every 25 pupils).

HMS Belfast is the last survivor of the Royal Navy's big ships whose main armanent was guns. Permanently moored in the Thames she is the first warship since *HMS Victory* to be preserved for the nation, her active career ending in 1963. Visitors may walk freely round the ship which has been preserved as nearly as possible in her original state. Areas open to the public include the operations room, messdecks (fitted out in traditional and more modern styles), sick bay, boiler room and engine room. There are special displays on naval gunnery, D-Day, and the development of the battleship.

Educational provision
Free worksheets at two levels (junior and secondary) are available along with a quiz sheet. During term time a programme of films at either junior, secondary or senior level can be arranged, and a slide show as well. Schools wishing these facilities should contact the Schools Officer in advance.

Refreshments
Kiosk is open in the summer during visiting hours selling snacks. There is a covered lunch area for school parties if booked.

Shop
Shop open during visiting hours sells booklets, postcards, wall charts and souvenirs.

BETHNAL GREEN MUSEUM OF CHILDHOOD

Cambridge Heath Road, London E2 9PA
Tel: 01-980 2415

Underground: Bethnal Green
British Rail: Cambridge Heath

Open
10 a.m. – 5.50 p.m. Mon to Thurs and Sat; 2.30 – 5.50 p.m. Sun.

Closed Fri, May Day, Christmas Eve, Christmas Day, Boxing
Day and New Year's Day.

Admission charges
Free.

The **Bethnal Green Museum of Childhood** has one of the
biggest toy collections in the world. Metal toys include cast
lead soldiers, farm figures and up-to-date spacemen as well as
little road vehicles such as Dinky toys. Toy locomotives are by
the great makers: Carette, Bing, Märklin, Lehmann and
Hornby. The teddy bears lead the collection of soft toys and
the most important paper toys are the board games ranging
from the historic 'Game of the Goose' to Monopoly. The Doll
collection begins with wooden dolls of early modern Europe
and includes dolls from Germany, and later French and
British dolls by famous 19th century makers. The collection
continues up to the Sindy and Sasha dolls of today. There is an
interesting collection of ethnic dolls, some using traditional
materials and some illustrating national costume such as the
dramatic Japanese warriors. The oldest and most precious
dolls' house is the Nuremberg house of 1673 and there are
many other fine pieces of miniature architecture. The
children's dress on display ranges from the present back to the
18th century.

Saturday workshops in the Art Room at 11 a.m. and 2 p.m.
are open to all children.

Special events
For details of future events, phone the museum.

Educational provision
A Teachers' Pack is available from the Education Department
of the Victoria and Albert Museum, London SW7 2RL
(tel: 01-589 6371).

Shop
Shop open 10.30 a.m.– 5.30 p.m. Mon to Thurs and Sat;
2.30 – 5.30 p.m. Sun, sells colour-cards, cut-outs, postcards,
posters, greetings cards, rag dolls, cut-out paper dolls and
paper scraps.

BEXLEY LONDON BOROUGH MUSEUM
(See Hall Place.)

BISHOPSGATE INSTITUTE
230 Bishopsgate, London EC2M 4QH
Tel: 01-247 6844

Underground: Liverpool Street
British Rail: Liverpool Street

Open
9.30 a.m. – 5.30 p.m. Mon to Fri.
Closed Sat and Sun.

Admission charges
Free.

The **Bishopsgate Institute** has local and travelling exhibitions from larger museums.

In 1985 there will be a mixture of exhibitions of photography and paintings. During the City festival in July it is hoped to have a photographic essay on Michael Tippett.

In September: City and Cripplegate Photographic Society Exhibition.
For future events, phone the Institute.

Refreshments
Cafeteria open 12 noon – 2.30 p.m. and vending machine sells tea, coffee, soup and hot chocolate.

BLAKE HALL GARDENS

Bobbingworth, Ongar, Essex CM5 0DG
Tel: 0277 362502

Underground: Epping

Open
Summer   10 a.m. – 6 p.m. Daily.
Winter   10 a.m. – 5 p.m. Daily.
Closed Christmas Day and New Year's Day.

Admission charges
Children   50p.
Adults   £1.
School Parties
children 50p teachers free.
Parties over 20 people
Adults   75p.

Blake Hall Gardens and the House have been the home of the
Cure family for nearly 200 years. Blake Hall is essentially an
agricultural estate consisting of four farms, now mostly arable,
and about a hundred acres of woodland. The pleasure gardens,
grounds and Tropical House are open to the public. The
gardens and woods contain many named plants and trees and
flowering shrubs. In Spring daffodils and flowering bulbs fill
the gardens. There are many fine examples of oak, horse
chestnut, beech, ash, holly as well as cedars, spruce, and
sequoia. Ongar and District Model Railway Club has a display
with a working scale model of the section of line between
Ongar Station and the now closed Blake Hall station as it was
during the first decade of this century when it was owned by
the Great Eastern Railway. For the plant enthusiast, the
Tropical House features a unique collection of plants
assembled by the present owner, including orchids and cacti.

Special events
For details of future events, phone Blake Hall Gardens.

Educational provision

Several worksheets are available and can be supplied to each pupil if required. On Mondays to Fridays the cafeteria can be used as a lecture room if not previously booked for a coach party.

Refreshments

Cafeteria open 10 a.m. – 5 p.m.

Shop

Garden Centre open during visiting hours sells normal garden centre merchandise plus sweets and small selection of souvenirs.

Disabled

Wheelchairs available. Pathways all accessible to wheelchairs.

BOMBER COMMAND MUSEUM

Grahame Park Way, Hendon, London NW9 5LL
(same site as RAF and Battle of Britain Museums)
Tel: 01-205 2266

Underground: Colindale

Open

10 a.m. – 6 p.m. Mon to Sat; 2 – 6 p.m. Sun.
Closed Christmas Eve, Christmas Day, Boxing Day, New Year's Day, Good Friday and May Day.

Admission charges

Children 50p.
Adults £1.
OAP 50p.
Groups of 20 and above
Children 25p.
Adults 75p.

The **Bomber Command Museum** contains a striking display of famous bomber aircraft including the Lancaster, Wellington and Vulcan. The Wellington is the only surviving example of 11,461 aircraft which were built. Another unique aircraft is the Halifax which was recovered from a lake in Norway. Tribute is paid to the 8th and 9th USAAF in the display of photographs and memorabilia set out in front of the famous Flying Fortress and the B25 Mitchell. The aircraft display is complemented by pavilions which hold exhibits, from small-scale models to a full-size reconstruction of the office of Sir Barnes Wallis, the famous aircraft designer and inventor of the 'Bouncing Bomb'.

Educational provision
Sample worksheets for children of both primary and secondary age, for duplication, may be obtained from the Education Officer. Short introductory slide talks can be given by prior arrangement with the Education Officer, on weekdays only between 10 a.m. – 12.30 p.m.

Refreshments
Self-service cafeteria open 10 a.m. – 5 p.m. Mon to Sat and 2 – 5 p.m. Sun. Children's menu on application. Picnic building seats 50.

Shop
Opens with the Museum and closes one hour earlier sells postcards, posters, aviation books, plastic kits, slides and souvenirs.

Disabled
All parts of the museum are accessible by wheelchair.

BOSTON MANOR HOUSE

Boston Manor Road, Brentford, Middlesex TW8 9JX
Tel: 01-570 7728 extension 3974 or 01-570 0622

Underground: Boston Manor

Open
Oct to May 2.30 – 4.30 p.m. Sat. Other times by arrangement.

Admission charges
Free (children must be accompanied by an adult).

Boston Manor House was built in 1622-23 and its fine state room has a Jacobean strapwork plaster ceiling of exceptional quality, dated 1623, and a fine mantelpiece. The oak staircase is topped by heraldic beasts. The house was enlarged in 1670 and partly redecorated around 1830. Externally, it is red-brick and gabled and stands in a small park. Conducted tours can be arranged.

Educational provision
A guidebook, photograph (postcard) and leaflet on the visit in 1834 of William IV and Queen Adelaide are available for teachers.

BRENT LODGE PARK ANIMAL CENTRE

Church Road, Hanwell, London W7
Tel: 01-579 2424 extension 3209

British Rail: Hanwell

Open
10.30 a.m. until half an hour before the Park closes Daily. Closed Christmas Day.

Admission charges
Children 10p.
Adults 20p.

Brent Lodge Park Animal Centre is situated within a conservation area in the Brent Valley at the end of Church Road, Hanwell, and is bounded on its southern and western sides by the River Brent. It has many mature trees and a substantial open grass area. There have been animals in the Park for many years and it is because of this that it was, and still is, known in the area as the 'Bunny Park'; more recently, the introduction of more exotic species has meant a greater variety and interest. These include: monkeys, marmosets, chinchillas, snakes, ducks, terrapins, frogs, lizards, spiders (including a bird-eating spider), locusts, stick insects and an alligator.

Educational provision
Worksheets and booklets are available and lecture rooms proposed for the future.

Refreshments
Cafeteria open most weekends.

Shop
Ticket Office open during Centre hours sells badges, car stickers and booklets.

Disabled
Toilets and access to all parts.

BRITISH CRAFTS CENTRE

43 Earlham Street, London WC2H 9LD
Tel: 01-836 6993

Underground: Covent Garden

Open
1–5.30 p.m. Mon, Wed, Fri; 1–7 p.m. Thurs; 11 a.m.–5 p.m. Sat.
Closed Bank holidays.

Admission charges
Free.

The galleries of the **British Crafts Centre** are used to fulfil two main purposes. Firstly there is a constant turnover of members' work that includes glass, rugs, lights, ceramics, fabrics, clothing, paper, metalwork and jewellery, selected from the most outstanding craftspeople currently producing in this country.

Secondly, there is a programme of special exhibitions that focus on innovations in the crafts.

At the Centre are represented many of Britain's best-established makers, as well as a growing number of promising, lesser-known ones.

Special events
Details of future events by post or phone.

Shop
Open 10 a.m. – 5.30 p.m. Mon to Wed, Fri; 11 a.m. – 5 p.m. Sat. Sells mixed selection of modern British crafts – ceramics, glass, rugs, jewellery, pottery, furniture, textiles and books and magazines on crafts and design.

Disabled
The ground floor is accessible to the disabled.

BRITISH MOTOR INDUSTRY HERITAGE TRUST

Syon Park, Brentford, Middlesex TW8 8JF
Tel: 01-560 1378

Underground: Gunnersbury
British Rail: Kew Bridge and Isleworth

Open
Mar to Oct 10 a.m. – 5.30 p.m. Daily
Nov to Feb 10 a.m. – 4 p.m. Daily.
Closed Christmas Day and Boxing Day.

Admission charges

Children 80p.

Adults £1.60.

OAP 80p.

Family £3.72 (2 adults and up to 5 children – under 5s free).

School Parties

Children 70p, Adults £1.40.

The **Motor Museum Heritage Trust** presents the largest collection of Historic British cars anywhere in the world. Over 90 vehicles are displayed, from the earliest 1895 Wolseley to the present day. On show are many unique prototypes, record-breaking cars plus sectioned vehicles and engines. Videos show the RAC Rally, and the London to Brighton Veteran Run. There is also a display of model British cars. During the summer months at weekends, there are free rides in vintage cars. The best months to visit are June to August.

Educational provision

There is a conference room and a children's school room and worksheets are also available.

Shop

Shop open in museum hours sells souvenirs and books.

Disabled

There are special parking facilities for the museum and there are no stairs.

BRITISH MUSEUM

Great Russell Street, London WC1B 3DG
Tel: 01-636 1555 extensions 510 and 511

Underground: Tottenham Court Road and Russell Square

Open
10 a.m. – 5 p.m. Mon to Sat; 2.30 – 6 p.m. Sun.
Closed Christmas Eve, Christmas period, New Year's Day,
Good Friday and May Day.

Admission charges
Free.

The **British Museum** is one of the greatest museums in the
world, showing the works of man from all over the world from
prehistoric to comparatively modern times. The Egyptian
section has mummies, pharaohs, animals and jewellery. The
Greek section has scenes from the Trojan Wars, athletics and
daily life. There are Roman mosaics and from Roman Britain
the Sutton Hoo Treasure. Other sections deal with China,
India, the Assyrians, Coins and Medals and Britain from
prehistoric times to Medieval and later.

Exhibitions
For details of future exhibitions, phone the Museum.

Educational provision
Illustrated teachers' notes are available and guides, checklists
of objects, and reading lists. Trails are designed for the 8-12 age
range on various topics. Introductory talks can be arranged
and films on subjects relevant to the collections are shown at
3.30 p.m. on Tuesdays to Fridays to the general public and
these can also be booked by school and college groups.

Refreshments
Coffee Shop open 10.30 a.m. – 4.15 p.m. Mon to Sat
and 3 – 5.15 p.m. Sun.

Shop
Two shops open 10 a.m. – 4.45 p.m. selling books, badges, posters, postcards, cut-outs and souvenirs.

Disabled
Access is good to almost all parts of the Museum and disabled visitors are asked to contact the Museum first. A leaflet giving full details of facilities is available from the Information Desks or by post from the Education Service.

BRITISH PIANO AND MUSICAL MUSEUM

368 High Street, Brentford, Middlesex TW8 0BD
Tel: 01-560 8108

Underground: Gunnersbury
British Rail: Kew Bridge

Open
Apr to Oct 2 – 5 p.m. Sat and Sun.
Closed Nov to Mar, weekdays.

Admission charges
Children   50p.
Adults   £1.50.
School Parties
£35 up to 40 maximum.

The **British Piano and Musical Museum** started as a player piano museum but now houses many other instruments. The guided tour lasts for over an hour and includes listening to many instruments. How they work and their history is explained and music rolls made many years ago by famous organists and pianists can be heard and compared. The orchestrions play themselves from music rolls sounding almost like full orchestras, playing overtures from operas or selections from popular classics and dance music.

This is a splendid opportunity to see and hear superb

pianos, organs, orchestrions, orchestrelles, music boxes, barrel organs and a Wurlitzer.

School parties should book in advance to visit on Tuesdays to Fridays in the afternoons or evenings. Any particular instrument may be heard by special arrangement.

Shop
Shop open during museum hours sells music rolls, records, cassettes, postcards, bookmarks and books.

Refreshments
There are no toilets and no space available for eating packed lunches.

BROMLEY MUSEUM

The Priory, Church Hill, Orpington BR6 0HH
Tel: 0689 31551

British Rail: Orpington

Open
9 a.m. – 6 p.m. Mon and Wed; 9 a.m. – 8 p.m. Tues and Fri;
9 a.m. – 5 p.m. Sat.
Closed Thurs and Sun.

Admission charges
Free.

The **Bromley Museum** houses local archaeological and historical collections, as well as geological specimens and ethnological exhibits. There are particularly interesting Roman and Saxon collections with Roman pottery, building materials, bricks and tiles, jewellery from habitation sites. The Saxon collection includes pottery, jewellery, weapons and skeletal remains from cemeteries.

Victoriana includes female and children's clothing and jewellery. The Avebury collection of antiquities and ethnography contains early pre-historic artefacts from all over

Europe, and from France, Denmark and England in particular.

The ethnographic section comes mainly from Oceania with models of canoes, weaponry, jewellery, carvings and deformed skulls. The museum also has a Queen Anne period fire engine.

Visiting groups are encouraged to work out their own projects.

Educational provision
The museum has a guide-curator and lectures can be arranged.

Disabled
There is easy access for wheelchairs and toilets for the disabled in the park surrounding the museum.

BRUNEL ENGINE HOUSE

St. Mary Church Street, Rotherhithe, London SE16
Tel: None

British Rail: Rotherhithe

Open
May to Sept 11 a.m. – 4 p.m. every Sun.
Oct to Apr 11 a.m. – 4 p.m. first Sun in each month.
Closed Mon to Sat.

Admission charges
Children   10p.
Adults   20p.
School Parties
by arrangement

Brunel Engine House was erected by Marc Isambard Brunel (father of Isambard Kingdom) for the Thames Tunnel – the first underwater tunnel in the world. Inside the engine house is a restored steam pumping engine and a display about the history of the tunnel.

Educational provision

Worksheets are in preparation and guides to the engine house are available for 10-20p from the engine house.

Shop

Sales Stand inside the engine house sells publications.

Disabled

Limited access within the building.

BURLINGTON HOUSE

(See Royal Academy of Arts.)

BUNKER, THE

(See Cabinet War Rooms.)

CABARET MECHANICAL THEATRE

33-34 The Market, Covent Garden, London WC2
Tel: 01-379 7961

Underground: Covent Garden

Open

10 a.m. – 8 p.m. Mon to Sat; 12 noon – 5 p.m. Sun.
Closed Christmas Day, Boxing Day.

Admission charges

Children 50p.
Adults £1.
Students and OAP 50p.
School parties advised to come term-time mornings. Charges are by arrangement.

The **Cabaret Mechanical Theatre** is the only collection of contemporary automata – working mechanical models – in this country. This permanent exhibition has a handful of models which require 10p or 20p but the majority (over 50 of them) can be worked by pushing a button or turning a handle. All the models were built in the last 5 years by West Country artists – Paul Spooner, Peter Markey, Ron Fuller, Tim Hunkin, Richard Windley and Mo and John Shears.

These very sophisticated models have all their mechanics exposed to view and appeal to all ages. Some have stories associated with them – references to other works of art and mythology. The largest is a 9-foot dragon and perhaps the most amusing is the automated cat, with eyes which swivel and ears that turn, as the milk in its saucer disappears then reappears again.

Educational provision
A sheet giving descriptions of how to make one of the models – Manet's Olympia – is available.

Refreshments
There are several cafeteria in Covent Garden and a wine bar next door to the Theatre.

Shop
Shop is open during visiting hours and sells hand-made objects, specially made for sale e.g. working models.

Disabled
There are steps down to the lower level.

CABINET WAR ROOMS

Clive Steps, King Charles Street, London SW1A 2AQ
Tel: 01-930 6961

Underground: Westminster
British Rail: Victoria, Waterloo, Charing Cross

Open

10 a.m. – 5.50 p.m. Tues to Sun, Easter Mon, Spring Bank holiday and Summer Bank holiday. Last admission 5.15 p.m. Closed Mon and New Year's Day, Good Friday, May Bank holiday, Christmas Eve, Christmas Day and Boxing Day. The rooms may be closed at short notice on State occasions.

Admission charges

Children   (5–16 yrs) £1.
Adults   £2.
OAP, Student, UB40   £1.

The **Cabinet War Rooms** comprise the most important surviving part of the underground emergency accommodation which was provided to protect Winston Churchill, his War Cabinet and the Chiefs of Staff of Britain's armed forces against air attacks during the Second World War. Situated beneath a slab of protective concrete, the rooms were in operational use from 1939 to 1945. On view are a suite of nineteen historic rooms, among them the Cabinet Room, the Transatlantic Telephone Room (from which Churchill could speak directly to President Roosevelt in the White House), the Map Room where information about operations on all fronts was collected, and the Prime Minister's Room which served as Churchill's emergency office and bedroom until the end of the war. The rooms contain equipment, machines, and furniture from their operational days.

Educational provision

A free guide for younger children is in preparation, and a comprehensive guide leaflet is issued to all visitors free.

Shop

Shop open during visiting hours sells specially designed souvenirs, war-time posters, postcards, books and educational packs.

Disabled

There is a lift and toilet for the disabled.

CARE OF BUILDINGS EXHIBITION

Hampton Court Palace, East Molesey, Surrey KT8 9BS
(postal address: Apartment 39, Hampton Court Palace)
Tel: 01-943 2277

British Rail: Hampton Court

Open
9.30 a.m. – 5 p.m. Mon to Sat; 12 noon to 5 p.m. Sun; (last
admission 4.15 p.m.).
Closed during the Christmas period.

Admission charges
Children   £1.
Adults   £1.
Student   £1.

The **Care of Buildings Exhibition** is operated by the Building
Conservation Trust, an independent educational charity
established to promote the better care of buildings of all types
and ages. Full size reproductions of parts of typical everyday
houses show how they are made, what can happen through
neglect and how to repair and maintain them. There is a
special section on Energy Conservation. The exhibition takes
about an hour to visit.

Educational provision
Introductory talks and a questionnaire are available and
school groups may have use of a lecture room. School groups
should be well conducted by teachers.

Refreshments
Restaurant in the Tilt Yard Gardens open every day from
Easter until the end of October for lunches from 12 noon to
3 p.m. Cafeteria open in winter 10.30 a.m. – 3.30 p.m. and
summer 10 a.m. – 5.30 p.m.

Shop
Shop in Hampton Court Palace open until half-hour before
closing time, sells guidebooks, postcards and souvenirs.

Disabled

Access is difficult – there are four staircases and difficult steps.

CARLYLE'S HOUSE (National Trust)

24 Cheyne Row, Chelsea, London SW3
Tel: 01-352 7087

Underground: Sloane Square
British Rail: Clapham Junction

Open
Apr 1 to Oct 31   11 a.m. – 5 p.m. Wed to Sun and Bank holiday
Mon.
Closed Mon, Tues, Good Friday and Nov to Mar.

Admission charges
Children   60p.
Adults   £1.20.

Carlyle's House was built in 1708 in the reign of Queen Anne,
and was the home of Thomas Carlyle from 1834 to 1881. The
furniture in the house all belonged to the Carlyle family, and
many of their keepsakes are on display as well. Also Carlyle's
books, papers and personal possessions can be seen.

The parlour, drawing room, Carlyle's study and his
bedroom are all open to view, and also a Victorian kitchen.

Disabled
The house is difficult for the disabled as there are many steps.
However, the staff are on hand to give all possible assistance.

CHARLES DICKENS CENTRE

(See Dickens Centre.)

CHARTWELL (National Trust)

Westerham, Kent TN16 1PS
Tel: (Edenbridge) 0732 866368

British Rail: Sevenoaks

Open

House and Garden *Apr to Oct* 12 noon – 5 p.m. Tues to
Thurs; 11 a.m. – 5 p.m. Sat, Sun, Bank holiday Mon.
House only *Mar and Nov* 11 a.m. – 4 p.m. Sat, Sun and Wed.
Closed Mon (except Bank holidays), Fri, Tues following Bank
holiday Mon, Dec to Feb and Aug 9th for sheepdog trials.

Admission charges

Children   £1.15.
Adults   £1.30.
School Parties
Children 90p on Tues morning.
Pre-booked parties are asked to come on Tues morning only.

Chartwell is the home in which Sir Winston Churchill lived,
worked and enjoyed his family life and friends from 1922 until
his death in 1965. The study where he wrote so many of his
books, articles and speeches, the dining room where the guests
and conversation sparkled, and the personal mementoes of a
long and full life remain as though he and his family could
return at any minute. His paintings are displayed throughout
the house.

In the garden, the wall he built himself, the fish pools and
black swans and the magnificent views of Kent combine with
the house to show his wide range of interests and
accomplishments.

Educational provision

Resource pack for teachers are available at 50p each.

Refreshments

Self-service restaurant open during visiting hours.

Shop

Shop open during visiting hours sells items relevant to the house with a good selection of books by and about Winston Churchill.

Disabled

Arrangements can be made for access to the front door by car. Small lift in the house will take smaller wheelchairs. Toilets in the car park. The garden is rather hilly.

CHELSEA PHYSIC GARDEN

66 Royal Hospital Road, London SW3 4HS
(public entrance in Swan Walk)
Tel: 01-352 5646

Underground:
British Rail:

Open

Apr to Oct 2–5 p.m. Wed, Sun and Bank holidays;
12 noon– 5 p.m. May 21-24.
Closed Oct to Mar.

Admission charges
Children £1.
Adults £1.50.
Students £1.
School Parties
£1 per head.

The **Chelsea Physic Garden** is the second oldest Botanic Garden in the country, founded in 1673 and only recently opened to the public. It comprises four acres densely packed with approximately 5000 plants, many rare and unusual. The garden displays plants from a wide range of habitats, and shows many fine species which are not generally available. The botanical family beds are arranged to demonstrate a

40

possible evolutionary sequence, and indicate relationships between plants. The beds show the diversity of form, structure and range within a plant family.

There are over 100 listed specimen trees, including the tallest olive tree in Britain from which 7 lb of fruit were harvested in December 1976. In addition there is a herb garden where culinary and medicinal herbs are cultivated. Plants of particular homeopathic interest are grouped together.

Educational provision
A lecture room is available for hire for visiting educational groups.

Refreshments
Tea is served on Sundays 3.15 – 4.45 p.m.

Shop
Shop open during visiting hours sells plants, guidebooks and postcards.

Disabled
Disabled visitors may enter the garden from 66 Royal Hospital Road.

CHELSEA ROYAL HOSPITAL MUSEUM

**Royal Hospital Road, Chelsea, London SW3 4SL
Tel: 01-730 0161 extension 203**

Underground: Sloane Square

Open
10 a.m. – 12 noon and 2 – 4 p.m. Mon to Sat; and Sun from April to Sept.
Closed Bank holiday weekends (Sat to Mon) and Sun from Oct to Mar.

Admission charges
Free.

41

These are famous Wren buildings built in 1682-1692 and include the interior of the Chapel, Great Hall and museum. The Ranelagh Gardens and South Grounds are also open to the public. On display are maps, prints, pictures, and plans connected with the Royal Hospital and medals and uniforms of Chelsea pensioners. Applications for visits should be made to the Adjutant who will arrange for an In-Pensioner guide to conduct the party.

Shop
Shop at the museum open during visiting hours sells postcards, Christmas cards (in season), brochure on the Museum and souvenirs.

CHESSINGTON ZOO

Leatherhead Road, Chessington, Surrey KT9 2NE
Tel: (Epsom) 037 27 27227

British Rail: Chessington South

Open
10 a.m. – 5 p.m. Daily.
Closed Christmas Day.

Admission charges
Children £1.85.
Adults £3.25.
OAP £2.25.
School Parties
Children £1.25, Adults £2.25.
Note: Prices lower from Nov to Mar.

Chessington Zoo is set in 65 acres of Surrey's finest countryside and contains a large collection of rare and exotic animals and birds. The Reptile House has big snakes, tarantulas, scorpions and an alligator. All the usual big animals – lions, tigers and elephants, are here. Pringle – a King

Penguin of television fame can be seen, and the Gibbons are also a great attraction. The Celebrity Bird Garden is one of the largest in the country and contains over 100 different species. During the summer season admission includes a non-animal circus and Cinema 2001.

Educational provision
Worksheets and questionnaires can be provided and a slide pack can be loaned. School parties can arrange a visit to the Children's Zoo and the pupils can touch and pick up the handleable snakes there.

Refreshments
Cafeteria and bar and several catering outlets open during visiting hours.

Shop
Three shops open during visiting hours selling postcards, gifts, souvenirs and novelties.

Disabled
All enclosures and houses are accessible to the disabled – there are ramps and special toilets.

CHILTERN OPEN AIR MUSEUM

**Newland Park, Gorelands Lane, Chalfont St Giles, Bucks.
Tel: (Chalfont) 02407 71117**

British Rail: Chalfont and Latimer, and Chorley Wood

Open
Easter to Sep 2 – 6 p.m. Sun, Wed and Bank Holidays.
Closed Oct to Easter, Mon, Tues, Thurs, Fri, Sat. Pre-arranged parties may be admitted at other times.

Admission charges
Children 50p.
Adults £1.
OAP 75p.

Parties
10% reduction if over 30 people – with leader free.
School Parties
50p per person.

Chiltern Open Air Museum is a collection of buildings which
have been dismantled from various parts of the Chilterns and
re-erected at the Museum, having been repaired and restored
to their original condition. The buildings range in age from the
early 16th century to late 19th century and they have been
carefully sited in order to preserve the atmosphere and
surroundings of their period. The Museum is set in 45 acres of
parkland and woodland.

There is a nature trail and adventure playground and guided
tours are given round the buildings and woodland.

Special events
Craft Fair, Sheepdog trials and a vintage car rally.
For further details, phone the Museum.

Educational provision
Worksheets and teachers' guides will be available in 1985 and a
small classroom in one of the exhibition buildings.

Refreshments
Cafeteria open during public visiting hours.

Shop
Shop open during public visiting hours, or by arrangement,
sells mementoes.

Disabled
There are toilets for the disabled.

CHISWICK HOUSE

Burlington Lane, Chiswick, London W4 2RP
Tel: 01-995 0508

British Rail: Chiswick

Open

Mar 15 to Oct 15   9.30 a.m. – 6.30 p.m. Daily.
Oct 16 to Mar 14   9.30 a.m. – 4 p.m. Wed to Sun.
Closed daily from 1 – 2 p.m. Mon and Tues in the winter,
and Christmas Eve, Christmas Day, Boxing Day and
New Year's Day.

Admission charges

Children   (under 16) 30p.
Adults   60p.
OAP and UB40   45p.
Free admission to monuments is granted to parties of students
receiving full-time education. Form AM 24 gives details and is
available from Area Office, English Heritage, Thames House
North, Millbank, London SW1P 4QJ (tel: 01-211 8828).
Free admission not available from Apr 1 to Sep 30.

Chiswick House was built by the architect and patron of the
arts, the third Earl of Burlington. He set a fashion with this
Italian-style villa which was to house his library and art
collections. The gardens, one of the first of their kind in
England, were landscaped by William Kent and other masters.

Educational provision

Details of free educational resources from Education Service,
English Heritage, Room 3/25, 15-17 Great Marlborough
Street, London W1V 1AF (tel: 01-734 6010 extension 810).

Shop

Ticket kiosk sells books, guides and souvenirs.

Disabled

Parking facilities. Exterior and ground floor only are
accessible.

CHURCH FARM HOUSE MUSEUM

Greyhound Hill, Hendon, London NW4 4JR
Tel: 01-203 0130

Open
10 a.m. – 1 p.m., 2 – 5.30 p.m. Mon, Wed to Sat; 10 a.m. – 1 p.m.
Tues; 2 – 5.30 p.m. Sun.
Closed Christmas Day, Boxing Day, New Year's Day,
Good Friday.

Admission charges
Free.

Church Farm House Museum is a 17th century farm-house set
in a small garden in the old village of Hendon. It contains
period furnished rooms: a kitchen (c. 1820) and a dining-room
(c. 1850). The attics, showing the construction of the roof, etc.,
may be viewed on request.

The museum stages a continuous programme of temporary
exhibitions – about six each year – on topics from local and
social history and the decorative arts. Smaller displays –
usually of local archaeological material – are held
concurrently.

Special events
For details of future events, phone the Museum.

Educational provision
Worksheets are sometimes available for the temporary
exhibitions. There is a free guide to the Museum kitchen, and
free brochures giving background information are produced
for most temporary exhibitions. Guidebooks to the Museum
and surrounding area are available from the Museum shop or
by post.

Shop
Shop open during Museum hours sells postcards, pamphlets,
Town trails, guidebooks and London Borough of Barnet Local
History Publications.

Disabled

Because of the age and nature of the building, access for the disabled is extremely difficult, and wheelchairs cannot be used.

CITY FARM

(See Kentish Town City Farm.)

CLISSOLD PARK ANIMAL ENCLOSURE

Leisure Services, Clissold Park, Green Lanes, London N4
Tel: 01-800 1021

Underground: Manor House

Open

7 a.m. to sunset Daily.
Never closed.

Admission charges

Free.

Clissold Park Animal Enclosure is in a public park of some 59 acres. Visitors view the animals from outside the enclosure. Inside are fallow deer, waterfowl, rabbits, peafowl, hens and exotic aviary birds. Visitors may feed the waterfowl with bread and the rabbits with greens.

Refreshments

Cafeteria open from 10 a.m. until dusk selling snacks.

Disabled

There are toilets for the disabled.

CLOCK MUSEUM

The Guildhall, Gresham Street, London EC2 2EJ
Tel: 01-606 3030

Underground: Bank or Mansion House

Open
9.30 a.m. – 4.45 p.m. Mon to Fri.
Closed Sun, public and Bank holidays and for public functions (visitors should phone to check in advance).

Admission charges
Free.

The **Clock Museum** houses the collection of clocks and watches owned by the Worshipful Company of Clockmakers. Lantern, pendulum, long-case ('grandfather' style) and wooden clocks, watches and marine chronometers are on view. Many are magnificently bejewelled, inlaid or enamelled. Unusual dial arrangements, fashionable in the late 17th century can be seen and a strange-looking clock kept wound by the pressure of Hydrogen gas generated by the interaction of zinc and sulphuric acid.

The collection also traces the quest for accuracy, particularly in marine chronometers, where Britain led the world in the latter part of the 18th century. Perhaps the proudest possession of the Clockmakers' Company is John Harrison's own replica of his large longitude watch which won a £20,000 government prize in 1765 and which, when tested by King George III himself, had an error of only 4 1/2 seconds in over ten weeks' trial time.

Disabled
There are three steps, but flat access can be arranged through the library door.

COMMONWEALTH INSTITUTE

Kensington High Street, London W8 6NQ
Tel: 01-603 4535 extension 283

Underground: High Street, Kensington

Open
10 a.m. – 5.30 p.m. Mon to Sat; 2 – 5 p.m. Sun.
Closed occasional days including Christmas Day, New Year's
Day, Good Friday and May Day.

Admission charges
Free.

The **Commonwealth Institute** has exciting displays on each of
the 49 Commonwealth countries, depicting their history,
geography, flora and fauna, arts and crafts and people's
day-to-day work and leisure activities. A quarter of the world
is under this roof and it is a rich reflection of our own multi-
cultural society.

Visitors can climb on a Canadian Skidoo or a Swaziland
tractor, work a hand water-pump, or relax and watch a
selection of audio-visual displays.

Special events
For details of future events, phone the Institute.

Educational provision
Free activity booklets and a very wide range of educational
programmes are available. Teachers can request the brochure
describing special events for schools.

Refreshments
Restaurant and coffee bar open from 10 a.m. – 4.50 p.m. Mon
to Sat. Coffee bar 2 – 5p.m. Sun. Also, there is a schools' dining
room which can be booked for eating packed lunches.

Shop

Shop open from 10 a.m. – 5.30 p.m. sells publications and artefacts from around the Commonwealth.

Disabled

Lift and toilets for the disabled and educational programmes can be specially devised to suit parties of disabled visitors with an emphasis on a tactile experience.

COURAGE SHIRE HORSE CENTRE

Cherry Garden Lane, Maidenhead Thicket, Maidenhead, Berks SL6 3QD
Tel: (Littlewick Green) 062882 3917

British Rail: Maidenhead

Open

Mar to Oct 11 a.m. – 5 p.m. Tues to Sun, Bank holiday Mons. Closed Mon and Nov to Feb.

Admission charges

Children 75p.
Adults £1.50.
School Parties
75p per person.

The **Courage Shire Horse Centre's** 'Gentle Giants' stand around 18 hands high and weigh about a ton. They were the war and work horses of yesteryear. Today the horses are used by Courage for publicity purposes and they appear all over the country at events such as major horse shows, galas and carnivals. A farrier can be seen shoeing the horses three times a week. As well as shire horses, there is a domestic animals' enclosure and a birds' enclosure. In the Display Room are leather and metal harnesses, photographs from the past and hundreds of prize rosettes won at major shows all over the country – some very recently.

Free guided tours may be booked in advance.

Educational provision
Teachers' guides and school project sheets are available.

Refreshments
Cafeteria open 11 a.m. – 4.30 p.m.

Shop
Shop open 11 a.m. – 5 p.m. selling a wide range of souvenirs connected with Shire Horses and the Centre.

Disabled
The Centre is fully equipped for the disabled including toilet and ramped entrances to all parts.

COURTAULD INSTITUTE GALLERIES

41 Gordon Square, London WC1H 0PA
Tel: 01-580 1015

Underground: Goodge Street and Russell Square
British Rail: Euston

Open
10 a.m. – 5. p.m. Mon to Sat; 2 – 5 p.m. Sun.
Closed Bank holidays, Easter, May Day, 3-4 days at Christmas, 1-2 days at New Year.

Admission charges
Children   50p.
Adults   £1.
OAP, Student   50p.
School Parties
Free, up to secondary level.

The **Courtauld Institute Galleries** have the Princes Gate Collection of Old Master paintings including the Master of Flemalle, a rare Triptych of the entombment of Christ and thirty paintings by Rubens, including *Landscape by Moonlight* and a portrait of the family of Jan Breughel the

51

Elder. It also houses the Samuel Courtauld Collection of Impressionist and post-Impressionist paintings which includes Monet's *Bar at the Folies Bergere*, Cezanne's *Card Players*, Seurat's *Young Woman Powdering Herself*, Gauguin's *Nevermore*, and Van Gogh's *Self-portrait with Bandaged Ear*.

Special events
For details of future exhibitions, phone the Galleries.

Educational provision
Talks for visiting educational parties can be arranged through the office (tel: 01-387 0370).

Shop
Sales desk open during the Galleries' hours sells catalogues, cards, slides, poster, prints and framed cards.

Disabled
There are no special facilities for the disabled though the lift is large and can easily accommodate a wheelchair.

CRAFTS COUNCIL

12 Waterloo Place, London SW1Y 4AU
Tel: 01-930 4811

Underground: Piccadilly Circus

Open
10 a.m. – 5 p.m. Tues to Sat; 2 – 5 p.m. Sun.
Closed Mon when special arrangements can be made for school parties to visit.

Admission charges
Most exhibitions are free, and all are free to school parties pre-booked for Monday visits.

The **Crafts Council** has between eight and ten exhibitions of contemporary and historical crafts each year. Above the galleries is an information centre with an extensive slide library, films, videotapes, the national register of craftspeople, The Crafts Council Index, leaflets and answers to crafts questions of all kinds.

Special events
For details of future events, phone the Council.

Educational provision
On Mondays only, special arrangements are made for school parties, (maximum 20, and outside the lunch hour), with a brief introductory talk to the exhibition plus a worksheet to help pupils look at and understand the work. Occasional practical workshops coincide with certain exhibitions. Organised visits last approximately 1 1/2 hours. Teachers' guides are also available and parties can use the lecture room (again, on Mondays only).

Refreshments
Coffee bar Tues to Sun.

Shop
Shop open during gallery hours selling publications and postcards.

CRICKET MEMORIAL GALLERY

Lords Ground, London NW8 8QN
Tel: 01-289 1611

Underground: St John's Wood
British Rail: Marylebone

Open

On match days during the cricket season 10.30 a.m. – 5 p.m.
Mon to Sat.
Closed Sun and non-match days except by prior arrangement.

Admission charges

Children 25p.
Adults 50p.
OAP 25p.
School Parties
Free if pre-booked.

The **Cricket Memorial Gallery** has numerous items relating to
cricket, including paintings, prints, trophies, famous balls and
bats (including those of W. G. Grace, Don Bradman, Walter
Hammond and Hobbs), and the Ashes. The Ashes commemorate the first occasion when Australia beat the English
team on its home soil. One of the bails was burnt, in response
to a mock *Times* obituary, and its ashes placed in a small
brown pottery urn. For nearly one hundred years this
miniscule urn has been the symbol by which the results of Test
matches between Australia and England are measured.

Educational provision

Special arrangements can be made for school parties, with film
shows and talks illustrated with slides. Conducted tours are
taken round the inside of the Pavilion, and round the 'Real'
Tennis Court where a game is usually in progress. The Curator
can supply pamphlets and recommend books which may be
helpful in preparing pupils for visits.

Refreshments

Snack bars are open during the season and the Lords Tavern
throughout the year.

Shop

Museum shop and MCC shops are open during visiting hours
selling a wide range of items of equipment and souvenirs.

Disabled

Some provision for the disabled can be made by arrangement beforehand.

CROSBY HALL

Cheyne Walk, London SW3 5AZ
Tel: 01-352 9663

Underground: Sloane Square and South Kensington

Open
10 a.m. – 12 noon, 2.15 – 5 p.m. Mon to Sat; 2.15 – 5 p.m. Sun.
Closed when previously booked for functions.

Admission charges
Free.

Crosby Hall was built by Sir John Crosby in 1466, part of a large medieval mansion in Bishopsgate. When the land was sold at the turn of the century for office development the Hall was removed and reconstructed in the garden of Sir Thomas More's Chelsea home, where it now is. The Hall features an inner roof of oak and chestnut, recently painted to bring it back to its medieval splendour, a delightful oriel and splendid fireplace. The floor is paved with Purbeck marble and there is a mounted Roman mosaic from the remains discovered underneath the original site in Bishopsgate.

CRYSTAL PALACE PARK CHILDREN'S ZOO

Crystal Palace Park, London SE20 8DT
Tel: 01-778 4487

British Rail: Crystal Palace or Penge West

Open
1.30 – 5.30 p.m. Mon to Fri; 11 a.m. – 6 p.m. Sat and Sun,

Bank holidays and School holidays.
Closed during the winter (beginning of October to first week of Easter).

Admission charges
Free.

Crystal Palace Park Children's Zoo has wallabies, monkeys, agouti, llamas, toucans, magpies, penguins, cranes, rheas, donkeys, ponies, sheep and goats. Special arrangements can be made to open the zoo for large parties on weekdays only in the mornings. For children under 12, pony rides are available.

Refreshments
Refreshment Bar is normally open from 10 a.m. in the summer season.

Disabled
All paths are accessible for wheelchairs.

CUMING MUSEUM

155-157 Walworth Road, London SE17 1RS
Tel: 01-703 3324

Underground: Elephant and Castle
British Rail: Elephant and Castle

Open
10 a.m. – 5.30 p.m. Mon to Wed, Fri; 10 a.m. – 7 p.m. Thurs;
10 a.m. – 5 p.m. Sat.
Closed Sun and Bank holidays.

Admission charges
Free.

The **Cuming Museum** preserves archaeological evidence for the local history of the Southwark area, and also specialises in London superstitions. The permanent display shows the story of the local community and its environment from desolate prehistoric riverside, through a small market town at the foot of London Bridge with its outlying villages, to the present industrial sprawl. Exhibits include: Roman sculptures, including a box for the ashes of a dead person found thrown down a well; and the water pump from the Marshalsea debtors' prison, alongside other items associated with Dickens' contacts with Southwark in his childhood and working life. There are the personalia of Michael Faraday, ceramic works by the artist George Tinworth, and milk delivery equipment from a turn-of-the-century local dairy. Amongst London superstitions is a sandwich, made in 1915, containing hair of a child with whooping cough to be given to a dog and so transfer the illness to the animal by magic!

Educational provision
Quiz sheets, drawing boards, stools and objects for handling are all available to school parties. Talk and/or demonstrations by the staff can be given by prior arrangement.

Shop
Small sales point open during museum hours sells a number of booklets and souvenir pencils.

Disabled
Information leaflets can be brailled for the blind. Wheelchair access to the museum is impossible as it is up a flight of stairs.

CUTTY SARK CLIPPER SHIP

**King William Walk, Greenwich, London SE10 9BL
Tel: 01-858 3445**

British Rail: Greenwich

Open

10.30 a.m.– 5 p.m. (6 in summer) Mon to Sat; 2.30 – 5 p.m.
(6 in summer) Sun and Good Friday.
Closed Christmas Eve, Christmas Day, Boxing Day and
New Year's Day.

Admission charges

Children (under 16) 50p.
Adults £1.
School parties (of 15 or more)
Children 25p.
Adults 50p.
Must be pre-booked and not Sat or Public holiday.

The **Cutty Sark** is the last remaining clipper ship in the world
and the most famous. She lies fully rigged as she would have
been in her sailing days. Built in 1896, her length is 212.5 feet,
beam 36 feet and tonnage 921 tons net. Her cargoes were China
Tea (1870-77) and Australian Wool (1883-95). She was given
to the Cutty Sark Society in 1953, and has had 9 1/2 million
visitors. Visitors may see over every part of the ship. The Cutty
Sark is an impressive and fascinating reminder of the grand
and dangerous days of sail, with many interesting relics on
board.

Visitors are also welcome to board the Gipsy Moth IV to see
how Sir Francis Chichester lived and the equipment he used.

Educational provision

Teacher's guide to the Cutty Sark, price £1.75, contains
worksheets which can be duplicated.

Shop

Shop open during visiting hours sells postcards, notebooks,
plans, books and souvenirs.

Disabled

Disabled can only visit the upper cargo hold.

DARWIN MUSEUM

Down House, Luxted Road, Downe, Orpington, Kent BR6 7JT
Tel: (Farnborough) 0689 59119

British Rail: Bromley South then 20 mins bus ride

Open
1 – 5.30 p.m. Tues to Thurs, Sat and Sun and Bank holiday Mons.
Closed Mon and Fri, Feb, Christmas Eve, Christmas Day and Boxing Day.

Admission charges
Children   30p.
Adults   £1.20.
OAP   60p.

Darwin Museum is housed in Down House, Darwin's home for 40 years from 1842. The property now belongs to the Royal College of Surgeons which has assumed the task of maintaining Charles Darwin's home as a memorial. The rooms open to the public are on the ground floor. The Old Study where most of his work was done is decorated and furnished almost as he knew it and the Drawing Room has been restored as closely as possible to its appearance when the family were in residence. Much of the furniture, pictures and many of the other exhibits are those in use during Darwin's lifetime. The former Dining Room is devoted to items relating to Charles Darwin himself and his work, and in the room opposite are displayed manuscripts, published works and other articles belonging to his grandfather Erasmus.

Outside the house, much of the garden remains as Darwin knew it. The 'Sandwalk' encloses a little wood planted by Darwin with various trees and taking in the summer-house and a pit out of which the sand was dug. This became the customary place of Darwin's daily exercise and was known as his 'thinking path' for here he planned his work as he walked.

Educational provision

Teachers are encouraged to make up their own worksheets from a preliminary visit.

Shop

Shop open during museum hours sells books, pens and postcards.

DAVID EVANS SILK PRINTERS

Bourne Road, Crayford, Kent DA1 4BP
Tel: 0322 57521

British Rail: Crayford or Bexley

Open

10.30 a.m.–4.30 p.m. Mon to Fri; 9. a.m.–12.30 p.m. Sat. Closed Sun and Bank holidays.

Admission charges

Free.

Note: Children under 14 are not allowed into factory areas.

David Evans Silk Printers was established in 1825 and is still in operation. A guided tour takes visitors around the silk workshops, showing the various stages of silk production, and both the traditional and new styles of silk printing. Tours start at 11 a.m. and 3 p.m. from Mon to Fri.

Educational provision

A video film about 15 minutes long shows hand block printing. There is a TV room with seating for 30 which teachers can use.

Refreshments

Vending machine sells coffee, tea, lemon and hot chocolate.

Shop

Shop open during visiting hours sells pure silk ties, scarves, silk by the metre, and craft items.

Disabled

There is access for the disabled.

DEEN CITY FARM

Batsworth Road, Mitcham, Surrey SW19
Tel: 01-648 1461

Underground: Colliers Wood

Open
10 a.m. – sunset Daily.
Never closed.

Admission charges
Children   10p.
Adults   10p.
Guided Tour   20p per child.

Deen City Farm has a variety of chickens, ducks and geese
wandering free in the farmyard. In the rabbit house there are
Angoras, Albino, Belgian Lop-Eared and a few Cavies. There
is a small herd of milking goats – British Saanen and British
Toggenburg, a Golden Guernsey kid and a very rare Old
English Goat kid, as well as sheep. In the riding school are two
Shetland Ponies, a Palomino, a Skewbald and a Black Welsh
cob. There is a Gloucester Old Spot pig with occasional
piglets, and sheep.

Visitors can try their hand at spinning, take a pony ride for
20p and if they have time there is always a job to be done on
the farm.

Educational provision
A classroom is available and worksheets. School parties can
have a guided tour with spinning and milking demonstrations.
Videos and incubators are for hire.

Refreshments
Canteen open 12 noon – 1.30 p.m.

Shop
Farm shop open at weekends and by request during the week,
selling fresh eggs, honey and assorted bric-a-brac.

Disabled
There are special toilets and raised gardens for the disabled
and a path runs the whole length of the farm and round some
of the buildings.

DE MORGAN COLLECTION

(See Old Battersea House.)

DESIGN CENTRE

28 Haymarket, London SW1Y 4SU
Tel: 01-839 8000

Underground: Piccadilly

Open
10 a.m.–6 p.m. Mon and Tues; 10. a.m.–8 p.m. Wed to Sat;
1–6 p.m. Sun.
Closed Christmas Day and Boxing Day.

Admission charges
Free.

The **Design Centre** provides continuing but changing
exhibitions of new developments in design in the consumer,
contract and engineering fields. Aimed at the public, trade
buyers, industrialists and people professionally interested in
design, the programme includes exhibitions on a variety of
subject or themes, and an annual review of all products
selected for The Design Centre during the previous year.

Special events
For details of future events, phone the Centre.

Educational provision
Worksheets and brief talks on the work of the Design Council available on request.

Refreshments
Cafeteria opens as above and closes 30 minutes before closing time.

Shop
Bookshop open during Centre hours sells design-oriented books. Shop also open during Centre hours sells kitchen equipment, stationery, glassware, ceramics, toys and goods from the exhibitions.

Disabled
There is a chair lift and escalator.

DICKENS CENTRE

Eastgate House, High Street, Rochester, Kent
Tel: (Medway) 0634 44176

British Rail: Rochester

Open
10 a.m. – 12.30 p.m., 2 – 5.30 p.m. (last admission 5 p.m.)
Daily.
Closed Jan 1, Good Fri and 4 days at Christmas.

Admission charges

Children   55p.
Adults   £1.
OAP   55p.
Parties   (20 or more)
Children   50p.
Adults   80p.
OAP   50p.
School Parties
50p per person.

The **Dickens Centre** consists of a series of galleries and rooms containing 'set piece' displays of scenes and characters from his books, together with Dickensian and biographical displays showing Dickens' development as a man and writer. These displays are imaginatively and dramatically executed so as to capture the imagination of the visitor and transport him to 19th century England as Dickens saw and recorded it. There is extensive use of sound and lighting effects and the Centre goes beyond the usual concept of a museum.

Special events
For details of future events, phone the Centre.

Educational provision
Junior and Senior worksheets are available free and these relate to the exhibition.

Shop
Shop open during centre hours sells pens, pencils, books, prints, posters, postcards, Dickens' works and souvenirs.

DICKENS HOUSE MUSEUM

48 Doughty Street, London WC1N 2LF
Tel: 01-405 2127

Underground: Russell Square

Open
10 a.m.– 5 p.m. (last admissions 4.30 p.m.) Mon to Sat.
Closed Sun and Bank holidays.

Admission charges
Children 50p.
Adults £1.
Student 75p.
Families £2.

The **Dickens House Museum** is the only London house still
standing that Charles Dickens lived in for any length of time.
He worked here on *Pickwick Papers, Oliver Twist, Nicholas
Nickelby* and *Barnaby Rudge*. There are some reconstructed
rooms where the young writer created some of his most
famous characters, and collections of manuscripts, drawings
and letters.

Educational provision
Information sheets and sample worksheets are available for
school parties. There are facilities for research.

Shop
Open during museum hours selling books, prints, charts,
stationery and Dickens souvenirs.

DISCOVERY

(See Historic Ship Collection.)

DORNEY COURT

**Dorney, near Windsor, Berkshire SL4 6QP
Tel: (Burnham) 06286 4638**

British Rail: Slough, Taplow and Windsor

Open

Easter to mid-Oct 2 – 5 p.m. Sun, Bank holiday Mons, Easter Sat.

June to Sept 2 – 5 p.m. Sun, Mon, Tues and Bank holiday Mons.

Closed mid-Oct to Easter.

Note: Parties of 20 or more welcome at other times by arrangement.

Admission charges

Children £1.
Adults £1.95.

Dorney Court is an enchanting, many gabled, pink brick and timbered Manor house, built about 1500 and lived in by the present family for nearly 400 years. The house is furnished with early 15th and 16th century oak, beautiful 17th century lacquer furniture, and 18th and 19th century tables. There are 400 years of family portraits, stained glass and needlework. The house is surrounded by fine formal gardens which are noted for their yew hedges.

Refreshments

Refreshments can be made available by arrangement and home-made cream teas are served.

Shop

Small souvenir shop specialises in home-grown vegetables and honey.

DULWICH PICTURE GALLERY

Gallery Road, Dulwich, London SE21
Tel: 01-693 5254

British Rail: North Dulwich and West Dulwich

Open

10 a.m. – 1 p.m. and 2 – 5 p.m. Tues to Sat; 2 – 5 p.m. Sun.
Closed on Mon.

Admission charges

Children (under 16) free.
Adults 60p.
OAP, Student 30p.
School Parties
Free.

Dulwich Picture Gallery is a small museum in a rural
environment. The John Soane gallery houses outstanding
collection of Old Master paintings. The 17th century masters
are represented by Poussin, Claude, Rubens, Van Dyck,
Teniers, Murillo, Rembrandt and many other Dutch Masters.
The 18th century is represented by Hogarth, Reynolds,
Gainsborough, Lawrence, Watteau, Tiepolo and Canaletto.
With 13 rooms and about 300 pictures on view, the Gallery is
on a pleasantly small scale and can easily be seen in an
afternoon.

Educational provision

School parties can be given talks, and worksheets, drawing
materials and teachers' notes are available. A seconded ILEA
teacher is available to work in schools and in the Gallery.
There are musical, dramatic and dance events for school
children who visit.

Shop

Shop open during gallery hours sells postcards, slides and gifts.

Disabled

The entrance to the museum is almost flat and assistance is
available. The gallery itself is totally flat. There are no special
toilets.

ELM FARM BATTERSEA

Gladstone Terrace, Battersea, London SW8 4BA
Tel: 01-627 1130

British Rail: Battersea Park and Queenstown Road

Open
8.30 a.m.–1 p.m. and 2–5 p.m. (please phone before coming).
Never closed.

Admission charges
Free but donations welcome.

Elm Farm is a newly established farm in the heart of the city.
Visitors are encouraged to phone before coming so that
arrangements can be made to involve them in the activities of
this farm. At present there is a small range of domestic farm
animals and a programme of expansion is planned for the
coming year to include workshops and play schemes.

Educational provision
The owners hope to expand classroom facilties in the near
future.

Refreshments
Snacks can be provided by prior arrangement.

Disabled
There is wheelchair access to the majority of the site and
toilets for the disabled.

ELTHAM PALACE GREAT HALL

Court Yard, Eltham, London SE9
Tel: 01-859 2112

British Rail: Mottingham and Eltham Well Hall

Open

Mar 25 to Oct 28   11 a.m. – 7 p.m. Thurs and Sun.
Oct 29 to Mar 24   11 a.m. – 4 p.m. Thurs and Sun.
Closed Mon to Wed, Fri and Sat.

Admission charges
Free.

Eltham Palace Great Hall was built by Edward IV and probably completed by the time of his death in 1482. It has the original hammer-beam roof – one of only three in the country. The Bishop of Durham developed the walls and moat in the 12-13th century and the first recorded royal guest, Henry III, visited the house in 1270. It was a principal royal residence from 1311-1547 but was ransacked in 1648 and the hall subsequently used as a barn. In the 1830s it was kitted out as a tennis court. In 1911 the Ancient Monuments Department repaired the wall, bridge and moat walls and in 1945 it was leased to the Royal Army Education Corps and the Hall is now used as an officers' mess.

Shop
Book table sells guides and postcards.

EPPING FOREST CONSERVATION CENTRE

High Beach, Loughton, Essex IG10 4AF
Tel: 01-508 7714

Underground: Loughton
British Rail: Chingford

Open

Easter to Oct 31   10 a.m. – 12.30 p.m. and 2 – 5 p.m. (or dusk if earlier) Wed to Sat; 11 a.m. – 12.30 p.m. and 2 – 5 p.m. (or dusk if earlier) Sun and Bank holidays.
Nov 1 to Easter   Sat and Sun only – times as above.
Closed

Summer Mon and Tues (but not Bank holidays).
Winter Mon to Fri, Christmas and the New Year.

Admission charges
Free.
The Centre runs courses and charges are made for these.

The **Epping Forest Conservation Centre** is a unique venture in
environmental education in the widest sense, providing
professionally tutored field studies for all levels of formal
education, weekend courses for adults, a base for ecological
research and interpretative and information service for the
general public. The Centre is situated at High Beach, in the
heart of the Forest. Public lectures are held once a month in
the winter on various aspects of historical, natural history and
conservation interest. An information desk in the Centre
supplies information to general visitors with displays about
the Forest. There is a monthly programme of guided walks.

Educational provision
The centre runs non-residential day courses – environmental,
geological and ecological – for school visitors from primary
level up to sixth form. There are courses for teachers and a
walk and talk service for young people. A teachers' pack is
available on request.

Shop
Shop open during Centre hours sells maps, postcards, guide
books, nature trail leaflets and souvenirs.

Disabled
There is a ramp into the information area.

EPPING FOREST MUSEUM

**Queen Elizabeth's Hunting Lodge, Rangers Road,
Chingford, London E4 7OH
Tel: 01-529 6681**

British Rail: Chingford

Open
2 – 6 p.m. (or dusk if earlier) Wed to Sun.
Closed Mon and Tues.

Admission charges
Children   free (must be accompanied).
Adults   20p.
School Parties
Free if booked.

Epping Forest Museum is housed in a timber-framed royal
hunting lodge built in 1543. Displays show the wildlife and
history of Epping Forest. On view are stuffed animals, birds
and other creatures, hunting weapons, traps and woodworking
tools.

Educational provision
Talks and guided tours are provided for schools and other
groups. These must be booked in advance.

Refreshments
Kiosk nearby in the forest selling light refreshments.

Shop
Shop open during visiting hours selling postcards, pamphlets
and maps.

EYNSFORD CASTLE

Eynsford, Kent
Tel: 0322 86 2536

British Rail: Eynsford

Open
Mar 15 to Oct 15   9.30 a.m. – 6.30 p.m. Mon to Sat;
2 – 6.30 p.m. Sun.
Oct 16 to Mar 14   9.30 a.m. – 4 p.m. Mon to Sat;
2 – 4 p.m. Sun.

Closed Daily from 1 – 2 p.m. and Christmas Eve, Christmas Day, Boxing Day and New Year's Day.

Admission charges
Children   (under 16) 15p.
Adults   30p.
OAP, UB40   20p.

Free admisison to monuments is granted to parties of students receiving full-time education. Form AM24 gives details and is available from Area Office, English Heritage, Thames House North, Millbank, London SW1P 4QJ (tel: 01-211 8828). Free admision not available from April 1 to September 30.

Eynsford Castle is a small Norman castle built shortly after 1066 as a consequence of the in-fighting between William the Conqueror's henchmen. It was held by seven successive William de Eynsfords, alike not only in name but also in being violent and quarrelsome. The castle was sacked in 1312 amid drunken revelry and has never been lived in since.

Educational provision
Details of free educational resources from Education Service, English Heritage, Room 3/25, 15-17 Great Marlborough Street, London W1V 1AF (tel: 01-734 6010 extension 810).

Shop
Ticket kiosk sells souvenirs, books and guides.

Disabled
Parking facilities, and the castle is accessible to the disabled.

FENTON HOUSE (National Trust)

Hampstead Grove, London NW3
(Postal: Windmill Hill, London NW3 6RT)
Tel: 01-435 3471

Underground: Hampstead

Open
Apr to Oct   11 a.m. – 6 p.m. Mon to Wed and Sat;
2 – 6 p.m. Sun.
Mar   11 a.m. – 6 p.m. Sat only.
Closed Thurs and Fri and from Nov to Feb.

Admission charges
Children   (under 17) 80p.
Adults   £1.60.
School Parties   80p per person.
National Trust members free.

Fenton House was built around 1693 in William and Mary style, and is one of the earliest and largest houses built in Hampstead, and one of the best architecturally. It houses one of the finest collections of English and Continental Porcelain with examples from Staffordshire, the Meissen factory, Bristol and Plymouth. The Oriental Room has a fine collection of Chinese porcelain which ranges in date from the 9th to the 18th centuries, and The Blue Porcelain Room is now given over to a display of blue and white Chinese porcelain, almost all of the K'ang Hsi period (1622-1722).

The collection of early keyboard instruments – harpsichords, spinets, and virginals – was acquired over a lifetime by Major Benton Fletcher. Serious students of the harpsichord can apply in advance to practice upon the instruments. There is a fine walled garden.

Special events
For details of future events, phone Fenton House.

FORTY HALL

Forty Hill, Enfield, Middlesex EN2 9HA
Tel: 01-363 8196

British Rail: Enfield Town

Open
Summer   10.00 a.m. – 6 p.m. Tues to Fri;
10 a.m. – 8 p.m. Sat and Sun.
Winter   10.00 a.m. – 4 p.m. Tues to Fri;
10.00 a.m. – 4 p.m. Sat and Sun.
Closed Mon.

Admission charges
Free.

Forty Hall is a Jacobean building, constructed in 1629 under
the impression of Inigo Jones. Its courtyard has an elaborate
entrance. Its permanent collection is of 16th and 17th century
furniture and it also houses a local history museum with
findings from Forty Hall lake and the surrounding area,
paintings of the region and fossils found in the Borough of
Enfield.

Special events
For future exhibitions, phone Forty Hall.

Refreshments
Cafeteria open during visiting hours. Children's meals can be
provided.

Shop
Shop open during visiting hours sells local postcards, history
material and badges.

FOUNDLING HOSPITAL ART GALLERY AND MUSEUM

40 Brunswick Square, London WC1N 1AZ
Tel: 01-278 2424

Underground: Russell Square
British Rail: Euston and Kings Cross

Open
10 a.m. – 4 p.m. Mon to Fri.
Closed Sat and Sun, Public holidays and when rooms are in use for Conferences, etc. Visitors are advised to check by telephone beforehand.

Admission charges
Children   10p.
Adults   30p.
School Parties
10p each.

The **Foundling Hospital Art Gallery** has on view about 120 paintings including works by Hogarth, Gainsborough and Reynolds. There are sculptures by Rysbrack and Roubiliac. Also on display are musical scores by Handel. There is a collection of mementoes of the foundling hospital.

Note: visits by parties of children under the age of 15 are not recommended unless they are studying Art or English Social History.

FREIGHTLINERS FARM

Sheringham Road, Islington, London N7
Tel: 01-609 0467

Underground: Highbury and Islington

Open
2 – 7 p.m. Tues to Fri; 9 a.m. – 1 p.m. and 2 p.m. – 7 p.m.
Sat and Sun.
Closed Mon.

Admission charges
Free

Freightliners Farm has cows, sheep, pigs, goats, rabbits,
guinea pigs, and a wide range of poultry: chickens, ducks,
geese, turkeys. Visitors can help in the small growing area and
also get involved in the day-to-day routine of the farm –
feeding, milking, mucking out and grooming.

Educational provision
A copy of worksheets for teachers to duplicate can be
supplied. If there are enough staff available, groups can be
accompanied and questions answered.

Disabled
There is ramped access to buildings but no special toilet
facilities.

GATWICK AIRPORT

Gatwick, West Sussex RH6 0NP
Tel: 01-668 4211 or 0293 28822

British Rail: Gatwick

Open
9 a.m. – 4 p.m. (viewing facilities) Daily.
Never closed.

Admission charges
Children   15p.
Adults   30p.
School Parties
Contact: 0293 503843.

From the **Spectators' Gallery** on the roof of the Arrivals Hall
visitors can watch airport activities, including aircraft landing
and taking off, cargo and maintenance facilities, and
construction of the North Terminal. Inside, are check-in
desks, shops and lounges.
Winter months are the best times to visit when the terminal
and spectators' areas are less crowded.

Educational provision
Information pack for school visits can be obtained by phoning
0293 503096 (Public Relations Department).

Refreshments
Several cafeteria are open for 24 hours. A number of
restaurants serve children's meals.

Shop
Several selling books, magazines, newspapers, sweets and
gifts. There is a craft stall selling various British crafts.

Disabled
There are toilet facilities for the disabled and a lift goes up to
the Spectators' Gallery. Terminals are fitted with ramps.

GATWICK ZOO AND AVIARIES

Rough Hill Road, Charlwood, nr Crawley, RH6 0EG
Tel: (Crawley) 0293 862312

British Rail: Gatwick.

Open
Easter to end of Oct   10.30 a.m. – 6 p.m. Daily.
Closed Nov to Mar.

Admission charges
Children   75p.
Adults   £1.50.
OAP   75p.
School Parties
10% reduction.

Gatwick Zoo and Aviaries has many small animals including monkeys, otters, wallabies and deer in a deer paddock. Wildlife can be seen here in a natural setting. A large number of birds include macaws, flamingoes, penguins and cockatoos. Visitors are able to picnic in the grounds. From Easter to the end of the summer there are always baby animals to be seen.

Educational provision
Questionnaire available for school children.

Refreshments
Cafeteria open 11 a.m. – 5 p.m.

Shop
Shop open 11 a.m. – 5 p.m. sells postcards, gifts and souvenirs.

Disabled
Access to all parts of the zoo and the cafe through rear door.

GEFFRYE MUSEUM

Kingsland Road, Shoreditch, London E2 8EA
Tel: 01-739 8368

Underground: Old Street
British Rail: Liverpool Street

Open
10 a.m. – 5 p.m. Tues to Sat; 2 – 5 p.m. Sun.
Closed on Mon (except Bank holidays), Good Friday,
Christmas Eve, New Year's Day.

Admission charges
Free.

The **Geffrye Museum** houses a collection of English furniture,
paintings and decorative arts, which span the period from
1600 to 1939, set out in period room settings. The development
of domestic design can be traced from a time when relatively
few people possessed movable furniture to one in which
consumer choice is available to a large proportion of the
population. The Museum's collection of paintings has been
formed principally to illustrate costume and aspects of social
life. The costume gallery in the Bradmore House Room was
opened in 1980. The exhibits, which represent only a selection
of the museum's holdings, complement the room settings and
the paintings collection.

Special events
For details of future events, phone the Museum.

Educational provision
In term-time there is a full schools' programme which
includes room talks with period costumes, project days and
extended talks to all age-groups. Pre-booking is essential
(tel: 01-739 9893).

In the holidays and half-terms there are projects and children's activities and these continue on Saturdays in term-time. The hours for these are 10 a.m. – 12.30 p.m. and 2 – 4 p.m. Children under 7 must be accompanied by an adult.

Refreshments
Coffee bar open 10.30 a.m. – 4.30 p.m.
(Lunch 12.40 – 1.40 p.m.).

Shop
Shop open during Museum hours sells books, postcards, children's items and catalogues.

Disabled
Facilities for the disabled include toilets, a ramp and access to most of the Museum except the upstairs 1930s room.

GENERAL CAB COMPANY MUSEUM

(See London Cab Company Museum.)

GEOLOGICAL MUSEUM

Exhibition Road, South Kensington, London SW7
Tel: 01-589 3444

Underground: South Kensington

Open
10 a.m. – 6 p.m. Mon to Sat; 2.30 – 6 p.m. Sun.
Closed Good Fri, 3 days at Christmas, New Year's Day, May Day.

Admission charges
Free.

The **Geological Museum** shows the formation of the earth
from its very beginnings. There are magnificent displays of
gemstones and fossils. Exhibits are also arranged in regional
and economic displays. A moving platform, with sound and
commentary, simulates the experience of being in an
earthquake.

Educational provision
For educational visits, worksheets are available at the
bookshop. Demonstrations, talks and film shows can be
arranged with the Education Department – application by
letter or phone.

Refreshments
Two vending machines selling hot and cold drinks.

Shop
Shop open during museum hours sells books, postcards,
jewellery, slides, specimens, maps, guides and souvenirs.

Disabled
There are special toilets for the disabled.

GEORGE INN (National Trust)

77 Borough High Street, Southwark, London SE1
Tel: 01-407 2056

Underground: London Bridge

Open
11 a.m. – 3 p.m. and 5.30 – 11 p.m. Mon to Fri;
11.30 a.m. – 3 p.m. and 6.30 – 11 p.m. Sat;
12 noon – 2 p.m. and 7 – 10.30 p.m. Sun.
Closed 4 days from Dec 21 and 4 days from Dec 30.

Admission charges
Free.
Note: There is a special room for children under the age of 18.

The **George Inn** is owned by the National Trust and is the only remaining galleried inn in London. Still open and operating as a public house, it was famous as a coaching terminus in the 18th and 19th centuries. Special features are the panelled walls, open fireplace and Parliament Clock, in the Old Bar. The Inn is mentioned by Dickens in *Little Dorritt.*

Refreshments
Wine Bar is open daily serving food 12 a.m. – 2 p.m. and 5.30 – 10 p.m. Two restaurants serve meals Mon to Sat. There is a small area for seating children.

GODSTONE FARM

Tilburstow Hill Road, Godstone, Surrey
Tel: Godstone 0883 842546

British Rail: Oxted, South Godstone and Redhill

Open
March 1 to end of Dec   10 a.m. – 6 p.m. Sat and Sun and Daily during school holidays.
Closed Jan and Feb.

Admission charges
Children   90p.
Adults   one free adult per child, otherwise 90p.
School Parties
95p per child. No charge for teacher or adult helpers (the price includes, lecture, demonstrations and questionnaires).

Godstone Farm is a 40 acre farm on the A22 near Godstone Village, 20 miles south of London. The land is mostly grass, surrounded by trees and with a stream running through it. The stock includes Dexter cattle, British Saddleback pigs, Shetland and Jacob sheep, goats, rabbits and a variety of chickens, ducks, geese and other poultry. Crops are grown in small demonstration plots, and there is a vegetable garden, fruit and Christmas trees. A cereal exhibit explains the various processes such as ploughing, drilling and harvesting. This includes plenty of facts and statistics for older children, and also a hand mill in which teachers can grind up a free sample of grain into flour.

A milk display shows milk production from grass to bottle, and a nature trail has been laid out.

In the shearing season demonstrations will be held every Sunday.

Educational provision
Lectures with colour slides are given in our lecture room. Demonstrations will be given, according to the season, of hand milking, sheep shearing, dosing, and dipping. Children will have a chance to handle some of the animals and feel such things as hay, wood, straw and corn. There are quiz and colouring sheets for younger children and questionnaires for older ones.

Shop
Shop open 10 a.m. – 6 p.m. sells coffee, eggs, postcards and farm books.

Disabled
Almost all of the farm is accessible to the disabled.

GPO SORTING OFFICE
(See Mount Pleasant Sorting Office.)

GRANGE MUSEUM OF LOCAL HISTORY
Neasden Lane, London NW10 1QB
Tel: 01-452 8311

Underground: Neasden

Open

12 noon – 5 p.m. Mon to Fri (Wed to 8); 10 a.m. – 5 p.m. Sat. Closed on Sun and Bank holidays.

Admission charges

Free.

The **Grange Museum of Local History** was built as the stable block of a substantial new farm some time between 1700 and 1709. A century later it was converted into a picturesque gothic cottage and it remained a private home until the last tenant died in 1971. It was repaired and converted in 1974-5 and opened to the public in May 1977. On display are a variety of everyday objects arranged to show aspects of local life in the past. Most of these objects have been given or lent by today's local residents. A Victorian parlour and a 1930s lounge represent the two main periods of house-building in the borough and a complete Edwardian draper's shop has been rescued and re-built in the museum. Other displays cover such topics as work, leisure, the home, transport and war.

Educational provision

An education officer will be appointed early in 1985 and provision will expand then. Courses are available for local teachers and a small room where special educational activities can be carried out, e.g. handling sessions on particular topics arranged in advance for visiting groups.

Shop

Shop open during museum hours sells badges, postcards, quiz sheets, local history and other historical publications at modest prices.

GREENWICH BOROUGH MUSEUM

(See Plumstead Museum.)

GREENWICH LOCAL STUDIES CENTRE

'Woodlands', 90 Mycenae Road, Blackheath, Greenwich,
London SE3 7SE
Tel: 01-858 4631

British Rail: Westcombe Park Station

Open
9 a.m. – 8 p.m. Mon, Tues and Thurs; 9 a.m. – 5 p.m. Sat.
Closed Sun, Wed and Fri.

Admission charges
Free.

Greenwich Local Studies Centre displays photographs,
postcards, prints, maps, archives and has local newspapers
and magazines on microfilm. Also on film are the 1841 to 1881
census returns for Greenwich. The centre has books,
pamphlets, posters, and commercial and street directories.

The Woodlands Art Gallery on the ground floor has
exhibitions of local artists and is open 10 a.m. – 7 p.m. Mon,
Tues, Thurs and Fri; 10 a.m. – 6 p.m. Sat and 2 – 6 p.m. Sun.

Educational provision
Talks, geared to the teacher's syllabus, and lectures are given
and worksheets provided. Pupils from 7 to 18 make use of the
centre as do college students.

Shop
Shop open during Centre hours sell printed matter and
illustrations.

Disabled
There is a wheelchair entrance to the Art Gallery and toilets in
the next building.

GUILDHALL

Gresham Street, London EC2P 2EJ
Tel: 01-606 3030

Underground: Bank or Mansion House

Open
10 a.m. – 5 p.m. Mon to Sat.
Closed on Sun, public and Bank holidays, and for public
functions (visitors should phone to check in advance).

Admission charges
Free.

The **Guildhall** has always been the heart of the City of London.
Civic activity and proud ceremonial have been centred here
for more than a thousand years. It has witnessed trials,
demonstrations, elections, receptions, banquets and the
conferment of the Freedom of the City ceremonies. It was
burnt in the Great Fire of 1666 though its walls remained, and
badly damaged in the Second World War. Twice
reconstructed, it has a magnificent porch with medieval
interior and gilt bosses. Seven medieval columns to north and
south, each formed by three clustered shafts, divide the hall
into three bays. The roof is the fifth to rest on the medieval
shafts and its stone arches, continuing the lines of the ribs of the
columns, carry the eye upward giving a powerful effect of
height and dignity.

    Statues of Gog and Magog have traditionally welcomed
visitors to the Guildhall and when they were destroyed in 1940
a new pair were carved by David Evans, standing
9 ft 3 ins high.

Disabled
Flat access by arrangement and then the whole Guildhall can
be seen.

GUINNESS WORLD OF RECORDS

The Trocadero, Piccadilly Circus, London W1V 7FD
Tel: 01-439 7331

Underground: Piccadilly Circus

Open
10 a.m. – 10 p.m. Daily.
Closed Christmas Day.

Admission charges
Children (under 16) £1.50.
Adults £2.50.
OAP £1.75.
Parties Children £1.25, Adults £2 (schools – 1 free adult with every 10 children).

The **Guinness World of Records** brings to life thousands of the amazing and varied facts from the world's most famous and successful publication, the *Guinness Book of Records*. There are six principal themed areas to the Exhibition: The Human World, The Animal World, Our Planet Earth, Structures and Machines, The Sport World, The World of Entertainment, and British Innovation and Achievement. Each section is a self-contained area which, using the latest display techniques, models, computers and audio visuals, recreates the superlatives featured in the *Guinness Book of Records*. Visitors can compare their height against the world's tallest man, watch Henri La Mothe dive into 12 3/8" of water, see the largest surviving litter of puppies – or at least the 15 that sat still for the photograph – and walk through the jawbone of a whale. They can weigh themselves next to the fattest man, listen to record-breaking songs and call up information on computers.

Educational provision
Worksheets are being compiled and will be ready by publication.

Refreshments
Cafeteria and restaurant open from 10 a.m. to midnight.

Shop
Shop open during visiting hours sells souvenirs of the exhibition.

Disabled
Wheelchair access has been arranged but advance booking, especially for groups, would be appreciated.

GUNNERSBURY PARK MUSEUM

Gunnersbury Park, London W3 8LQ
Tel: 01-992 1612

Underground: Acton Town

Open
Mar – Oct (to end of BST)   1 – 5 p.m. Mon to Fri; 2 – 6 p.m. Sat, Sun and Bank holidays.
Oct (from end of BST) – Feb   1 – 4 p.m. Mon to Fri; 2 – 4 p.m. Sat, Sun and Bank holidays.

Admission charges
Free.

Gunnersbury Park Museum was formerly a private country residence owned by the Rothschild Family. The purpose of the Museum is to illustrate how local people have lived in the past in the areas now covered by the London Boroughs of Ealing and Hounslow. The collections are particularly strong in archaeology, transport (including two Rothschild carriages), Acton laundry material and domestic life. Other groups include: ceramics, costumes, dolls, furniture, jewellery, maps, postal, and weapons. The number of items within each group varies considerably; only part of the collections are on display at any one time but schools can arrange to view items in store by prior appointment. The Victorian Rothschild kitchens are at present under restoration but there will be limited opening: June to September by arrangement for schools groups – Tuesdays and Thursdays, also open during the last weekends in September.

Exhibitions
For future events phone the Museum.

Educational provision
If pre-booked at least 2 weeks in advance, staff can give introductory talks (about 45 minutes) with objects (some for handling) from the Museum's reserve collection and slides – maximum 15 children. Guides can take school groups around and some worksheets are available together with help for teachers making their own.

Refreshments
Cafeteria in the park open daily from April to September and winter Saturdays and Sundays in fair weather.

Shop
Shop open during museum hours sells inexpensive publications on the museum collections and local history, and some souvenirs.

Disabled
The displays are all on the ground floor and accessible by wheelchair.

HACKNEY CITY FARM

1A Goldsmith's Row, London E2
(office at St Chad's Vicarage, Duncoe Street, London E2)
Tel: 01-729 4854/6381

Underground: Old Street
British Rail: Liverpool Street

Open
Usually open during normal working hours.
Official opening mid-October 1985.

Admission charges
Free – donations welcome.

Hackney City Farm was set up by a group of people who felt strongly that vacant land should be put to good community use and decided to convert a one-and-a-half acre derelict site into a city farm. The site was originally a brewery and the intention is to blend agriculture and horticulture with the site's industrial past. This is a new project and during the summer of 1985 the farm will acquire animals, stock gardens, and begin a programme of special events including traditional craft demonstrations and social events.

Visitors can help with gardening, building, animal husbandry and other activities, subject to discussion.

Educational provision
Talks can be given on various subjects – for example ecology, community management and growing.

Refreshments
Light refreshments are available by arrangement.

Shop
A shop will open to sell farm produce, animal masks, plants, etc.

Disabled
Access to garden area and ground floor level of the farm.

HALL PLACE

Bourne Road, Bexley, Kent DA5 1PQ
Tel: (Crayford) 0322 526574

British Rail: Bexley

Open

Winter   10 a.m. – 4.15 p.m. Mon to Sat.
Summer   10 a.m. – 5 p.m. Mon to Sat; 2 – 6 p.m. Sun and
most Bank holidays.
Closed Winter Sun, Christmas Eve, Christmas Day, Boxing
Day, New Year's Day and Good Friday.

Admission charges

Free.

Hall Place is a part-Tudor, part Jacobean country house on
the outskirts of Bexley village. The present house dates back to
about 1540, but there is evidence of earlier houses on this site
as far back as 1241. Stonework from the 13th to the 15th
centuries is found in the walls, much of it medieval mouldings.
In the 17th century the moulded plaster ceiling in the North-
West wing was constructed, and it is regarded as one of the best
of its period in Kent. The house has been extensively restored
this century and is now the Headquarters of the Bexley
Borough Libraries and Museums Service. It houses a Local
Studies Centre which has archives, local history documents,
Kent collections, Local History collections, photographs and
microfilms of local newspapers.

Educational provision

Worksheets are often available for exhibitions. Pre-arranged
visits can be made to the Local Studies Centre as can guided
tours for parties.

Refreshments

In the summer a cafeteria is open outside Hall Place.

Shop

Sales desk open during visiting hours sells various
publications and pamphlets and postcards produced by the
Local Studies Section.

HAM HOUSE (National Trust)

Ham, Richmond, Surrey
Tel: 01-940 1950

Underground: Richmond
British Rail: Richmond

Open
Oct – Mar 12   12 a.m. – 4 p.m. Tues to Sun.
Apr – Sept   2 – 6 p.m. Tues to Sun.
Closed Mon.

Admission charges
Children   75p.
Adults   £1.50.
OAP, UB40 and *pre-booked groups*   75p.
School Parties
Free

Ham House was built in 1610 and lived in at the time by the
Duke and Duchess of Laudersdale. It has original interiors
and furniture of the period, re-creating life at the time of the
Royalists and Roundheads. It has a fine restored 17th century
formal garden and rose garden.

Refreshments
Cafeteria open from April to September.

Shop
Open from April to September selling National Trust goods.

Disabled
There are toilet facilities and wheelchairs are available.

HAMPTON COURT PALACE

East Molesey, Surrey KT8 9AU
Tel: 01-977 8441

British Rail: Hampton Court

Open

State Apartments

Oct 1 – Mar 31   9.30 a.m. – 5 p.m. Mon to Sat; 2 – 5 p.m. Sun.

Apr 1 – Sept 30   9.30 a.m. – 6 p.m. Mon to Sat; 11 a.m. – 6 p.m. Sun.

Last admission is half-hour before closing time.

Mantegna Paintings Gallery

As for State Apartments except in winter when closing time is either 5 p.m. or half-hour before dusk, whichever is earlier.

Great Kitchens and Cellars, Tudor Tennis Court, Kings Private Apartments and Hampton Court Exhibition

Apr – Sept only   Times as State Apartments

Gardens

Every day until dusk but not later than 9 p.m.

Maze

Mar and Apr   10 a.m. – 5 p.m. Daily.

May – Sept   10 a.m. – 6 p.m. Daily.

Oct   10 a.m. – 5 p.m. Daily.

Closed

The Palace (but not the Gardens) is closed New Year's Day, Good Friday, Christmas Eve, Christmas Day and Boxing Day. The Maze is closed from Nov to Feb.

Admission charges

State Apartments

Oct 1 – Mar 31	Children	(under 16) 60p.	
	Adults	£1.	
	OAP	60p.	
Apr 1 – Sept 30	Children	£1.	
	Adults	£2.	
	OAP	£1.	

Maze

25p per person.

The Gardens, Kitchens, Cellars, Tudor Tennis Courts and Hampton Court Exhibition are free of charge.

Parties   (11 or more) can obtain 10% discount on the day of the visit.

School Parties

May obtain special free permits from Oct – Mar (apply to School Party Bookings at the Palace address).

Hampton Court Palace was Cardinal Wolsey's country house, begun in 1514 and surpassing in splendour many a royal palace. Not surprisingly Henry VIII at first coveted and then obtained it prior to Wolsey's fall from power. Henry enlarged it; Charles I lived in it as King and as prisoner; Charles II repaired it; and William and Mary extended and partially rebuilt it to a design by Sir Christopher Wren. The beauty of Wren's buildings is combined with some of the finest Tudor architecture in Britain. In the palace are superb tapestries and furniture, and Venetian paintings by Titian, Tintoretto and Veronese. The magnificent wrought-iron gates were made by Tijou.

There are two guided tours each day (except Sundays) in summer (May to September) at 11.15 a.m. and 2.15 p.m. A complete tour takes approximately 1¹/₂ hours and no extra charge is made provided an entrance ticket to the State Apartments is held. Audio guides are also available in summer.

Refreshments
Restaurant in the Tilt Yard Gardens open every day from Easter until the end of October for lunches from.12 noon – 3 p.m. Cafeteria open Oct to Mar 10.30 a.m. – 3.30 p.m. and April to Sept 10 a.m. – 5.30 p.m.

Shop
Shop in the Palace open until half-hour before closing time sells guidebooks, postcards and souvenirs.

Disabled
Toilets and lift for wheelchairs but note uneven cobblestones and flagstones and gravel paths in the formal gardens.

HATFIELD HOUSE
Hatfield, Herts AL9 5NQ
Tel: (Hatfield) 070 72 62823

British Rail: Hatfield

Open
Mar 26 to Oct 13 12 noon – 5 p.m. Tues to Sat; 2 – 5.30 p.m. Sun.
Closed Mon except Bank holidays, Good Friday and Oct 14 to March 25.

Admission charges
Children £1.80.
Adults £2.45.
Parties of 20 or more booked in advance
Children £1.55.
Adults £2.
School Parties
£1.55 per child. One teacher free with 15 children.

Hatfield House was built as the Cecil family residence in 1607-11 and it has remained their home to the present day. The 6th Marquis of Salisbury now lives here. There are family portraits by the great painters of the day, including Reynolds and Richardson. There are two portraits of Elizabeth I – the Ermine portrait by Nicholas Hillyard and the Rainbow portrait thought to be by Isaacs. The fine furniture collected by the family represents various periods. The rare tapestries include early 18th century pieces made in the Sheldon factory in Warwickshire. Historic armour comes from England, Germany and Spain – possibly from the Armada. Relics of Elizabeth I include hats, gloves and stockings and in the garden is preserved the original oak tree which she was sitting under when she was brought news of her accession to the throne.

Special events
For details of future events, phone Hatfield House.

Educational provision
School parties can be given a guided tour by experienced guides.

Refreshments
Cafeteria open during visiting hours.

Shop
Three shops open during visiting hours sell gifts, souvenirs and plants.

HAYES HILL FARM

Crooked Mile, Waltham Abbey, Essex
Tel: 099 289 2291

British Rail: Waltham Cross

Open
10 a.m. – 6 p.m. (or dusk if earlier) Daily.
Never closed.

Admission charges
Children 55p.
Adults 80p.
School Parties
40-55p per person.

Hayes Hill Farm has all types of domestic animals – pigs, sheep, ponies, horses, rabbits, ducks, donkeys and cattle. There are both domestic and rare breeds – e.g. Longhorn, Highland and Dexter cattle. The animals are in pens and small paddocks where visitors can get close to and touch them. Visitors can also go into Holyfield Hall – a working dairy farm where cows are milked every day at 3 p.m. At harvest time combine harvesters can be seen in action.

On most Sundays in the summer there are craft demonstrations e.g. shoeing or thatching.

Educational provision
Worksheets, farm studies and colouring pictures for the very young.

Refreshments
Tea and coffee available throughout the day, are supplied free of charge.

Shop
Shop open 10 a.m. – 4 p.m. sells tea, coffee, ices, sweets and souvenirs.

HAYWARD GALLERY

South Bank, London SE1
Tel: 01-928 3144

Underground: Waterloo or Embankment
British Rail: Waterloo

Open
10 a.m. – 8 p.m. Mon and Tues; 10 a.m. – 6 p.m. Thurs to Sat;
12 noon – 6 p.m. Sun.
Closed for changeovers between exhibitions and for Public holidays.

Admission charges
Vary for each exhibition. Parties booked at least two weeks in advance can get considerable reductions.

The **Hayward Gallery** was built by the GLC and is maintained and run directly by the Arts Council as a venue for major national and international art exhibitions. It was opened in 1968.

Special events
For details of future events, phone the Gallery.

Educational provision
The Gallery has a full-time Education Officer, Jacky Percy, seconded by the ILEA. She is able to visit schools and arrange introductions to the exhibitions. Teachers' pack is also available, with notes for each exhibition.

Refreshments
Coffee Bar open 10.30 a.m. – 7.30 p.m. Mon and Tues;
10.30 a.m. – 5.30 p.m. Thurs to Sat and 12.30 – 5.30 p.m. Sun.
There is seating outside in good weather if the sculpture court is not being used for an exhibition.

Shop

Shop open during gallery hours sells postcards, posters, carefully selected books relevant to the exhibitions (at various prices) and a few selective gifts.

Disabled

Wheelchairs are available, and most of the Gallery is accessible. Disabled visitors should park in the car park and ring for an attendant and they will then be brought up in the lift.

HEATHROW AIRPORT

British Airports Authority, Queen's Building, Heathrow Airport, Hounslow, Middlesex TW6 1JH
Tel: 01-745 7224

Underground: Heathrow Central

Open

The Roof Gardens are open Daily from 10 to dusk.
Closed Christmas Day and Boxing Day.

Admission charges

Children   20p.
Adults   50p.
OAP   20p.
Disabled   free.

Heathrow Airport's Spectators' Roof Gardens have ample space from which to view, at close hand, the activity around aircraft on the parking aprons just below. The runways are clearly visible. Two are normally in use simultaneously, one for landings and one for take-offs.

Refreshments
Buffet open daily until half-hour before closing time.

Shop
Shop open from 10 a.m. – 3 p.m. sells postcards, books and souvenirs.

Disabled
Lift takes disabled visitors to the Roof Gardens.

HERALD'S MUSEUM at the TOWER OF LONDON

HM Tower of London, London EC3N 4AB
Tel: 01-236 9857 or 01-584 0930

Underground: Tower Hill

Open
Apr to Sept   9.30 a.m. – 5.45 p.m. Mon to Sat (last admission 5 p.m.); 2 – 5.30 p.m. Sun (last admission 4.30 p.m.).
Closed Oct to Mar, Good Friday and May Day.

Admission charges
Entrance fee included in Tower of London charges.

The **Herald's Museum at the Tower of London** was opened in 1980 to display some of the magnificent treasures collected by the Royal Heralds over the centuries. The main aim of the Museum is to explain what heraldry is about and to trace its development over the centuries. The second aim is to show some of the best examples of applied heraldry including: heraldic manuscripts, and heraldry used on glass, precious metals, porcelain, textiles and other artefacts. Part of the exhibition is changed every year to highlight the various aspects of heraldry. Permanent exhibits include crowns and crests of past Knights of the Garter, shields, banners showing the arms of various famous men, and the figure of a herald in uniform – as worn on State Occasions.

Educational provision
Various educational facilities and events are arranged by the Tower of London.

Shop
Shop open during museum hours sells souvenirs of heraldic interest.

Disabled
The Museum is accessible for wheelchairs.

HEVER CASTLE

Hever, Edenbridge, Kent TN8 7NG
Tel: (Edenbridge) 0732 865224

British Rail: Hever

Open
June, July and Aug   12 noon – 6 p.m. (last entry 5 p.m.) Daily.
Mar 31 – Oct 6   12 noon – 6 p.m. (last entry 5 p.m.) Fri to Wed; 12 noon – 6 p.m. Bank holidays.
Closed Oct 7 to Mar 30 and Thurs in Apr, May and Sept.

Admission charges
Gardens and Castle
Children £1.25.
Adults £2.75.
Gardens only
Children 75p.
Adults £1.50.
Party rates Gardens aBd Castle
Children 01.
Adults £2.25.
Gardens only
Children 75p.
Adults £1.20.
School Parties
50p per child, teachers free.
Special private tours for pre-booked parties on Thurs and any
evening – details on request.

Hever Castle dates back to about 1270 when the massive
Gatehouse, the outer walls and the moat were first
constructed. Two hundred years later the Bullen (or Boleyn)
family added a comfortable Tudor dwelling-house inside the
walls, and in the early 1900s, William Waldorf Astor restored
the Castle and built the astonishing 'Tudor Village' which lies
behind it and created the world-renowned gardens and lake.

Anne Boleyn was almost certainly born here, and here it
was that Henry VIII came to woo her for three years until he
was free to marry her. Memories of Anne Boleyn are
everywhere in Hever Castle: portraits, a bed-head, an
embroidered headdress, the prayer book she carried on her last
walk to the executioner's block in 1536. William Waldorf
Astor filled the Castle with the best craftsmanship he could
find – the finest furniture, pictures and objects d'art from the
Tudor and later periods, and always with spectacular displays
of fresh flowers – a tradition still continued.

The gardens were created in 1903-6 from rough, swampy
ground and are now at full maturity. The thirty acres are
backed by a beautiful tree-bordered 35-acre lake, and contain
separate areas of Spring garden, formal Italian garden, Rose

garden, Topiary garden and Woodland garden. In early Spring Hever is a mass of daffodils. Rhododendrons are at their height in May, and the Rose garden shows its best in June. The autumnal colouring throughout the gardens is famous. There are fountains and cascades everywhere, particularly in the area of the Italian garden, built as a backcloth to the unique collection of Roman and Classical statuary and sculpture and with its world-renowned Pompeiian Wall.

In the gardens is a fine maze, plus an adventure playground and a fleet of radio-controlled model boats for children of all ages.

Educational provision
Junior and senior worksheets available on request.

Refreshments
Cafeteria open 12 noon – 5 p.m.

Shop
Shop open 12 noon – 5.30 p.m. sells guide books, postcards, gifts and souvenirs.

Disabled
Toilets and ramps all the way round the Castle.

HISTORIC SHIP COLLECTION and *DISCOVERY*

St Katherine's Dock, London E1 9LB
Tel: 01-481 0043

Underground: Tower Hill
British Rail: Fenchurch Street

Open
Summer   10 a.m. – 5 p.m. Daily.
Winter   10 a.m. – 4 p.m. Daily.
Never closed.

Admission charges
Children 80p.
Adults £1.60.
OAP 80p.
Party rates to be arranged.

The **Historic Ship Collection** is a fleet of unique British
vessels, both sail and steam, from the late Victorian times
onwards. It includes Captain Scott's famous ship, *Discovery*,
built for him in 1900-1901 for his first expedition to Antarctica,
and now under restoration. The collection includes a further
six historic ships, barges, coasters and a light ship. Until
recently these vessels were berthed in various parts of the
country. They are now brought together and give an
opportunity for the public to see superb, and in some cases
unique, examples of a by-gone era at sea – an era known to
most only as pictures on a television or film screen. Here, in
this magnificent setting adjacent to the Tower of London,
visitors are free to walk amongst, and go aboard, ships that
portray the complex evolution from sail to steam and the way
ships have been adapted for specific tasks. Printed information
accompanies the displays, and a guide can be arranged if
necessary.

Educational provision
Information can be provided for teachers and a guide for
school parties.

Refreshments
Cafeteria open 10 a.m. – 4 p.m.

Shop
Shop open 10 a.m. – 4 p.m. selling coffee, biscuits and
souvenirs.

Disabled
Access to the ships is via steps and gangway and therefore not
suitable for the disabled.

HOGARTH'S HOUSE

Hogarth Lane, Chiswick, London W4
Tel: 01-994 6757

Underground: Turnham Green

Open
11 a.m. – 4 p.m. Wed to Mon.
Closed Tues, the first two weeks in Sept and three weeks in December.

Admission charges
Free.

Hogarth's house contains a permanent exhibition of Hogarth's engravings. The house, in 18th century Queen Anne style, is extremely unpretentious and pleasant, reflecting his quiet, honest life style. This was Hogarth's country retreat, in a quiet village, although nowadays it is in the middle of a conurbation. Hogarth's famous engravings, including *The Rake's Progress* and *Gin Lane* are on display here, along with scenes of 18th century London life in every aspect. The remainder of the tiny village can be reached with a short walk. As a contrast, the Palladian Villa, Chiswick House is only 400 yards away.

HORNIMAN MUSEUM

100 London Road, Forest Hill, London SE23 3PQ
Tel: 01-699 2339/1872/4911

British Rail: Forest Hill

Open
10.30 a.m. – 6 p.m. Mon to Sat; 2 – 6 p.m. Sun.
Closed Christmas Eve, Christmas Day and BoxingDay (except for the Director's lecture on Boxing Day).

Admission charges
Free.

The **Horniman Museum** has large permanent displays on
Natural History, ethnography, musical instruments and a
large aquarium/vivarium. The ethnography section is
arranged geographically and includes artefacts from all round
the world showing everyday life from the past and present,
including Egyptian mummies, and contemporary material
from Africa and Oceania. There is a large display of masks
from around the world. Other displays are arranged to show
animal defences, locomotion and evolutionary processes with
several stuffed animals – walrus and ostrich, and exotic and
domestic birds. The vivarium has snakes and lizards and there
is a sectional beehive where visitors can see into the hive and
its working bees.

Special events
For details of future events, phone the Museum.

Educational provision
The Education Centre is open weekdays during term-time.
Informal talks are given on a variety of museum topics,
illustrated by demonstration material, slides or films. All ages
and abilities are welcome, including groups from special
schools. Information sheets are available for teachers.

Refreshments
Tea-room open 1.30 – 4.30 p.m. Mon to Fri during term-time
and 11.30 a.m. – 4.30 p.m. during school holidays; 11.30 a.m. –
5.30 p.m. Sat; 2.30 – 5.30 p.m. Sun. These times are likely to
change during the year.

Shop
Shop open 10.30 a.m. – 4.30 p.m. Mon to Fri; 10.30 a.m. –
5.30 p.m. Sat and 2 – 6 p.m. Sun selling books, postcards,
posters, pens, pencils and souvenirs.

Disabled

The disabled can enter via the ground floor or via the Gardens to the upper floor by arrangement.

HOUSE OF ST BARNABAS

1 Greek Street, Soho Square, London W1
Tel: 01-437 5508

Underground: Tottenham Court Road

Open
2.30 – 4.15 p.m. Wed; 11 a.m. – 12.30 p.m. Thurs.
Closed Fri to Tues, Christmas and Easter weeks.

Admission charges
Free.
Note   children must be accompanied by an adult.
School parties
up to 25 and adult parties up to 30 welcome, after written pre-arrangement.

The **House of St Barnabas** is the last remaining house to preserve the magnificent and noble decorations of 18th century Soho Square, and has fine contemporary carving and rococo plaster work. The beautiful modelling of the plaster work is best seen on the principal staircase. The ceiling of the Council Chamber is a masterpiece of its kind. The Crinoline staircase is of special interest. The interior owes its beauty to the exceptionally good taste of its first owner, Richard Beckford.

The chapel was completed in 1863 and is built in the classical style of late 13th century French Gothic. The garden has a 300-year-old mulberry tree planted by Hugenots.

The house has been used since 1846 to help the destitute and homeless poor in London, and is still a residence for homeless women today.

Educational provision

Children may make sketches under adult supervision. A guide to the House can also be present.

HOUSEHOLD CAVALRY MUSEUM

Combermere Barracks, Windsor, Berks
Tel: (Windsor) 07535 68222 extension 203

British Rail: Windsor

Open

9.30 a.m. – 12.30 p.m. and 2 – 4.30 p.m. Mon to Fri. Also
Summer   10 a.m. – 4 p.m. Sun.
Closed Sat through the year and Sun in winter.

Admission charges
Free.

The **Household Cavalry Museum** has full-dress uniforms, equipment and weapons of the Household Cavalry from 1660 to the present date. There are swords, rifles, revolvers, helmets and a very good display of medals, as well as various colour standards, paintings of the lifeguards and a set of silver drums. Armoured cars include a Daimler, Saladin, Ferret and Daimler scout cars with a Panhard armoured car brought back from the Falklands.

HOUSES OF PARLIAMENT TOUR

London SW1A 0AA
Tel: 01-219 4750 (for further information)

Underground: Westminster

Open

By appointment with Peers and MPs only, and giving at least 6 weeks notice on sitting days.

107

10 a.m. – 12 noon Mon to Thurs; 3.30 – 5.30 p.m. Fri.
Summer recess by prior arrangement with an MP or Peer.
August   10 a.m. – 12 noon Wed, Thurs.
Sept   10 a.m. – 12 noon Tues, Wed, Thurs.
If the House of Commons rises in July, then July rules follow those of August.
Closed on these non-sitting days: Sat, Sun, Bank holidays and Good Friday, Christmas recess until the end of the New Year holiday; Summer recess except as above and except for parties of less than 6 personally escorted by an MP or Peer who can be admitted up to 5.30 p.m.

Admission charges
Free, but parties requiring the services of a guide (who must be pre-booked through an MP or Peer) will be charged approximately £8 per party of 16. Teachers may show their parties round themselves, provided they have a Member's permit. No party should exceed 16 in number.

The **Houses of Parliament Tour** takes visitors from the Norman Porch up the Royal Staircase, where the Queen enters for the State Opening of Parliament, into the Robing Room where she is dressed and then into the splendid Royal Gallery. The Royal Gallery has a model of Parliament as it was in Henry VIII's time, documents, and portraits of the Queen and her predecessors, together with statues of past monarchs e.g. Queen Elizabeth I and William the Conqueror. The tour then goes to the Prince's Chamber dominated by a statue of Queen Victoria and with many portraits of 16th century monarchs: Henry VIII, Edward, Mary and Elizabeth I.

Parties then pass through the Chamber of the House of Lords and the Peers' Lobby, and proceed through the central Lobby and Members' Lobby, passing the Whips Offices – the very important centres of party management. Visitors then go through the same doorway used by Black Rod when he knocks three times at the State Opening of Parliament and pass through the 'No' lobby where they learn how Members vote in a division.

After pausing in the Commons Chamber, visitors pass

through St Stephen's Hall, on the site of St Stephen's Chapel, where the Commons met for 300 years. And then into Westminster Hall, built originally by William Rufus in the 11th century, with its splendid 14th century wooden hammer-beam roof with carved angels. This Hall was the scene of the trials of Charles I and of Guy Fawkes – the Law Courts were here until the 1870s, and this is where recent monarchs have lain in state. The Hall is used for ceremonial occasions like the Queen's Jubilee Address.

Educational provision
A limited number of parties of senior schoolchildren can be shown an audio-visual presentation about Parliament's work. Between mid-September and mid-October this is shown every day as an integral part of a special course for fifth and sixth formers, run by the Education Officer. The application form for this 'Autumn Visits Programme' is published each Spring in the *Times* Educational Supplement. On sitting days a small number of gallery tickets are set aside for use by educational parties. Leaflets and wallcharts are available from the Education Officer.

Shop
Bookstall open generally when the Line of Route is open, sells tourist booklets, postcards and a number of larger books on Parliament's work.

Disabled
The disabled follow a modified Line of Route, and toilet facilities are available in the lower waiting hall.

HUNTERIAN MUSEUM

Royal College of Surgeons, Lincolns Inn Fields, London WC2A 3PN
Tel: 01-405 3474

Underground: Holborn

Open

Sept to July   10 a.m. – 5 p.m. Mon to Fri
Closed Aug, Sat, Sun and Public holidays.

Admission charges

Free
Admission by written application only. No children under 14 admitted.

The **Hunterian Museum's** collection was founded by John Hunter (1728-1793) to demonstrate comparative anatomy and physiology of living organisms, including foetal development, experiments in bone growth, the structure, development and diseases of teeth. Hunter's study of gross changes in the body (morbid anatomy) due to disease or trauma laid the foundations of modern pathology. Many of Hunter's experiments on animals and man made major contributions to the development of surgical technique. Although primarily arranged as a teaching collection for his surgical pupils, it contributed to the advancement of veterinary science.

Educational provision

The museum is primarily for medical students but parties of senior school pupils (preferably studying 'A' Level Biology) are welcome. An introductory leaflet for teachers is available.

Shop

A guide, price 50p, is available.

IBA BROADCASTING GALLERY

70 Brompton Road, London SW3 1EY
Tel: 01-584 7011

Underground: Knightsbridge

Open

Mon to Fri for guided tours starting at 10 a.m., 11 a.m. 2 p.m. and 3 p.m. Advance booking essential.
Closed Sat, Sun and Bank holidays.

Admission charges
Free. Minimum age limit of 16 years.

The **IBA Broadcating Gallery** was established at its London
headquarters in 1968. Visitors joining the 90-minute guided
tours are first given an introduction to the UK broadcasting
system and the growth of television throughout the world. The
second section shows the progression from early still
photography through moving pictures and 'persistence of
memory' to the cinema, telegraphy and eventually the
transmission of radio and television signals. The expansion of
television and its commercial aspects are explained, and a
demonstration of ORACLE teletext transmission leads visitors
on to a final multi-screen presentation and a glimpse of the
future. The gallery features many other areas of interest
including audience research, and the use of satellites.

Educational provision
The gallery tour has proved particularly valuable to schools
and colleges engaged in early stages of courses on
communications, the media, and other related subjects.

Disabled
Disabled individuals can be shown round by arrangement.

IGTHAM MOTE

Ivy Hatch, Sevenoaks, Kent
Tel: (Sevenoaks) 0732 62235

British Rail: Sevenoaks (6 miles from station)

Open
Mar – Oct   2 – 5 p.m. Fri.
Nov – Feb   2 – 4 p.m. Fri.
Apr – Sept   2 – 5 p.m. Sun.
Closed Mon to Thurs and Sat.

Admission charges
Children £1.
Adults £1.50.
Parties of 20 plus
Children 80p.
Adults £1.30.

Igtham Mote is a beautiful medieval moated manor house with important later additions. Features include the Great Hall, Old Chapel and Crypt *circa* 1340, Tudor Chapel with painted ceiling *circa* 1520, Drawing Room with Jacobean fireplace and frieze, 18th century Palladian window and hand painted Chinese wallpaper.

IMPERIAL COLLECTION

Central Hall, Westminster, London SW1
Tel: 01-222 0770

Underground: St James' Park and Westminster

Open
Feb – Nov 10 a.m. – 6 p.m. Mon to Sat.
Nov – Feb 11 a.m. – 5 p.m. Mon to Sat.
Closed Sun.

Admission charges
Children £1.
Adults £2.
School Parties
75p with one free per 20 persons.

The **Imperial Collection** is the authentic replica collection of the Royal, and Imperial Crown Jewels. Every piece is executed with complete accuracy and the result is a beautiful display of hand-set stones, perfect in size, facets, shape, colour and settings. The collection also includes regalia from Russia,

France, Persia, the Vatican and Hungary, a unique record of each country's heritage. Here are replicas of the most famous diamonds – the Cullinan, the Koh-I-Noor, and many others.

A guided tour round the collection takes about one hour.

Educational provision
Guide sheets and explanatory notes are available.

Refreshments
Restaurant open from 12 a.m. – 6 p.m. also serves children's meals (these must be booked separately).

Shop
Shop open in visiting hours sells postcards, books and crown jewels in miniature.

IMPERIAL WAR MUSEUM

Lambeth Road, London SE1 6HZ
Tel: 01-735 8922

Underground: Lambeth North and Elephant Castle
British Rail: Elephant Castle and Waterloo

Open
10 a.m. – 5.50 p.m. Mon to Sat; 2 – 5.30 p.m. Sun.
Closed Christmas Eve, Christmas Day, Boxing Day,
New Year's Day, Good Friday and May Bank holiday.

Admission charges
Free.

The **Imperial War Museum** has exhibits relating to the two World Wars and other aspects of 20th century history: tanks, aircraft, uniforms, medals, documents, paintings, posters, artillery, photographs, ephemera, and models. Displays illustrate military, political, social and cultural aspects of war.

There are quiz sheets for holiday visits and free film shows at weekends and during school holidays.

Special events 1985
For details of future events, phone the Museum.

Educational provision
The Museum has two teaching rooms with a programme of
talks arranged, and a large cinema with daily film shows. Free
worksheets and documents packs are available, and there are
sixth-form conferences, study days, courses for teachers,
occasional drama projects and other special events. Visits
must be pre-booked. There is a mailing list service for schools
wishing to receive regular information, and booklists can be
provided for children working on school projects.

Refreshments
Vending machines selling hot and cold drinks and
confectionery are in operation until 5 p.m.

Shop
Shop open during Museum hours sells postcards, facsimile
posters, hard and soft-cover books, slides and souvenirs.

Disabled
There are special toilets for the disabled and special access can
be provided for groups by arrangement.

INSTITUTE OF CONTEMPORARY ARTS

The Mall, London SW1
Tel: 01-930 3647

Underground: Piccadilly Circus and Charing Cross
British Rail: Charing Cross

Open
12 noon – 11 p.m. Tues to Sun.
Closed Mon.

Admission charges
50p for a day pass for the exhibitions. No charge for children
under 14.

The **ICA** runs an international programme of exhibitions in its three galleries. It runs a Cinema Club for children with occasional matinees in term-time, and the screenings are often accompanied by special guest speakers.

Special events
For details of future events, phone the Institute.

Educational provision
Special visits to the galleries can be arranged and any of the ICA Programme Directors (Visual Arts, Cinema, Theatre, Talks) are willing to talk to groups by prior arrangement.

Refreshments
Cafeteria open 12 noon – 8 p.m.

Shop
Shop open 12 noon – 9 p.m. selling books, catalogues, magazines, postcards and posters.

Disabled
Access to Main Gallery and Concourse, and lift to Upper Gallery. Prior arrangement preferable.

IVEAGH BEQUEST, KENWOOD
Hampstead Lane, London NW3 7JR
Tel: 01-348 1286/7

Underground: Archway or Golders Green

Open
Apr – Sept   10 a.m. – 7 p.m. Daily.
Feb – Mar and Oct   10 a.m. – 5 p.m. Daily.
Nov – Jan   10 a.m. – 4 p.m. Daily.
Closed Christmas Eve, Christmas Day and Good Friday.

Admission charges
Free.

The **Iveagh Bequest, Kenwood** combines great paintings, architecture and furniture. Robert Adam remodelled Kenwood for Lord Mansfield in the neo-classical style from 1764 and also designed much of the interior decoration and furnishings including the magnificent Library. The paintings are world famous and include the heroic late *Self Portrait* by Rembrandt, *The Guitar Player* by Vermeer and Gainsborough's portrait of the haughty Lady Howe. There are paintings by Van Dyke, Cuyp, Turner, Reynolds, Romney and Frans Hals. The growing collection of English 19th century furniture is in keeping with the style of the house, and a number of Adam pieces from America, including the original furniture have been added recently. There are also collections of 18th century shoe buckles and jewellery and some sculpture including the Piranesi Vase.

Educational provision
Introductions to the House and paintings can be made by appointment (Ms Gene Adams, ILEA Centre for Learning Resources tel: 01-633 2751/2).

Refreshments
Restaurant in the Coach House and restaurant in the Old Kitchen open during visiting hours.

Shop
Shop open during visiting hours sells postcards, reproductions, books and souvenirs.

Disabled
Toilets and wheelchair access – no steps.

JASON'S TRIP

Opposite 60 Blomfield Road, Little Venice, London W9
Tel: 01-286 3428

Underground: Warwick Avenue
British Rail: Paddington

Open
Easter – Oct   Daily.
Closed Nov to Mar.

Admission charges
Children   £1.25.
Adults   £2.25.
OAP   (Mon to Fri) £1.25.
School Parties
£1 plus one free place per 30.

Jason is an original, brightly painted, narrow boat built in 1906. It preserves all the colour and tradition of the English waterways, with painted cabin, fancy ropework and shining brass. It starts its 1 1/2 hour journey from Little Venice and travels along the Regent's Canal, around Brownings Island (named after the poet), through Maida Hill Tunnel under Blow Up Bridge and into London Zoo. It then continues past houses designed by Nash, the New Mosque, Primrose Hill and the Pirates Castle to Camden Lock, at which point it returns.

Educational provision
Worksheets can be supplied on request and a commentary is given on the journey which can be altered to suit special groups.

Refreshments
Cafeteria and vending machines open 9.30 a.m. – 6.30 p.m. selling tea, coffee, soft drinks and sweets. Sandwiches can be arranged if pre-booked.

Shop
Open from 9.30 a.m. – 6.30 p.m. selling cards and souvenirs.

Disabled

There are no special facilities for the disabled, but they can be taken on the trip if advance notice is given.

JENNY WREN CANAL CRUISES

250 Camden High Street, London NW1 8QS
Tel: 01-485 6210 and 01-485 4433

Underground: Camden Town

Open
Mar – Oct   11 a.m. – 2.30 p.m. (advance booking advisable)
Daily.
Closed Nov to Feb.

Admission charges
Children   £1.
Adults   £1.75.
OAP   Mon to Fri £1.
School Parties
85p per person.

A traditionally designed and decorated canal boat takes public trips along the most picturesque length of Regent's Canal. It travels from Camden Town Lock through the Zoo, Regent's Park and then via the canal tunnel to Maida Vale, around the island at 'Little Venice' and returns. These boats were the commercial and passenger carriers of the 17th and 18th century and used to ply along the whole of England's 4,000 miles of waterways. A commentary which can be geared to all age groups is given on the journey with descriptions of the canal, the boats, and their history. There is good weather protection aboard.

Disabled
Disabled groups are accepted for the trips.

JEWEL TOWER, WESTMINSTER

Old Palace Yard, London SW1
Tel: 01-211 8828

Underground: Westminster
British Rail: Victoria

Open
Oct 16 – Mar 14   9.30 a.m. – 4 p.m. Mon to Sat.
Mar 15 – Oct 15   9.30 a.m. – 6.30 p.m. Mon to Sat.
Closed Sun, Christmas Eve, Christmas Day, Boxing Day and
New Year's Day.

Admission charges
Free.

The **Jewel Tower** is one of the last remaining parts of the
Palace of Westminster. King Edward III built this moated
tower to store his personal jewels and all were sold by the boy
king Edward IV, after which the building became a storehouse
for the proliferating papers of the House of Lords and, later,
the Weights and Measures Department. On the top floor are
the old weights – bushels and copper weights – and liquid
measures.

   Also on display are shards of pottery found when the moat
was excavated and wooden piles (stakes) which were the old
foundations of the Palace of Westminster. Some fine Norman
capital heads can also be seen.

Shop
Sales counter open during visiting hours sells postcards,
guidebooks and souvenirs.

JEWISH MUSEUM

Woburn House, Upper Woburn Place, London WC1H 0EP
Tel: 01-388 4525

Underground: Euston
British Rail: Euston

Open

10 a.m. – 4 p.m. Tues to Thurs (and Fri in Summer);
10 a.m. – 12.45 p.m. Sun (and Fri in Winter).
Closed Mon and Sat.

Admission charges

Free.

The **Jewish Museum** specialises in Jewish ritual art and in the
history of the Jewish community in England before 1900.
Some of the notable objects are : a 16th century gilded and
carved walnut wood synagogue Ark from Italy, a 1734 Sabbath
lamp by Abraham Lopes de Oliveyra, a collection of 17th
century wedding rings, some fine illuminated Italian Marriage
contracts, and a collection of portraits and miniatures. Also,
presented to the Lord Mayors of London by the Spanish and
Portuguese synagogue during the 18th century, is a silver
salver and two silver cups.

Educational provision

Two tape and slide audio/visual programmes can be shown.
These are on Judaism and are designed for secondary school
religious education students.

Refreshments

There are no cafeteria, but Tavistock Square is a good place to
picnic in the summer.

Disabled

There is flat access and lifts.

JOHNSON'S, DR HOUSE

17 Gough Square. London EC4A 3DE
Tel: 01-353 3745

Underground: Temple, Chancery Lane, Blackfriars

Open
Oct to April 11 a.m.– 5 p.m. Mon to Sat.
May to Sept 11 a.m. – 5.30 p.m. Mon to Sat.
Closed Sun and Bank holidays.

Admission charges
Children 50p.
Adults £1.

Dr Johnson lived in many houses in London and this is the only one that survives. Here he compiled his great Dictionary of the English Language, published in 1755 and a first edition is on display. The house now contains portraits, letters and objects relating to Dr Johnson and his circle which included Burke, Burney, Elizabeth Carter, Garrick, Goldsmith, Reynolds and the Thrales. The house was built around 1700, panelled with American white and yellow pine, and contains original 18th century furniture.

Educational provision
An introductory talk with the opportunity to put questions can be arranged for visiting school parties. The trustees emphasise that this would be suitable for senior pupils and students pursuing literary or historical studies; the museum being unsuitable for small children.

Shop
Sales desk at the reception is open during visiting hours selling postcards, catalogues, prints and souvenirs.

KEATS HOUSE

**Wentworth Place, Keats Grove, Hampstead,
London NW3 2RR
Tel: 01-435 2062**

Underground: Hampstead or Belsize Park
British Rail: Hampstead Heath

Open
10 a.m. – 1 p.m. and 2 – 6 p.m. Mon to Sat;
2 – 6 p.m. Sun, Easter, Spring and Late Summer Bank
holidays.
Closed Christmas Day, Boxing Day, New Year's Day, Good
Friday, Easter Eve and May Day.

Admission charges
Free.

Keats House was built in 1815-16 and he lived here until his
death in 1821. The exterior of the house remains very much as
it was then and the mulberry tree on the front lawn probably
dates from Stuart times but the old plum tree, beneath which
Keats wrote his famous *Ode to a Nightingale* has been
replaced. Inside the house the poet's sitting room is practically
unchanged: it retains the original windows with their folding
shutters and the shelves on which Keats kept his books. The
house has been fortunate in receiving many relics of Keats and
these are displayed in the Brawne rooms and the Chester
Room. The Keats Memorial Library contains an extensive
collection of material relating to Keats and his
contemporaries. It includes microfilm copies of the Keats
manuscripts and material at Harvard University and of the
material in the Keats-Shelley Memorial House in Rome.

Educational provision
A guided tour can be given if arranged in advance – limit 25
persons – the visitors should have some knowledge of Keats
i.e. most suitable for 'O' or 'A' level students.

Shop
Sales point selling books and souvenirs.

Disabled
This house is not very suitable for disabled visitors as it is a
listed building on three floors with no lift.

KENTISH TOWN CITY FARM

1 Cressfield Close, Grafton Road, London NW5
Tel: 01-482 2861

Underground: Chalk Farm or Kentish Town

Open
10 a.m. – 5.30 p.m. Daily.
Closed Christmas Day.

Admission charges
School parties
30p per person. Otherwise free.

Kentish Town City Farm has cows, sheep, pigs, goats, rabbits
and poultry. Horses and ponies are of all sizes and ages and
pony rides (50p) are given at 2.30 p.m. on Sundays. According
to the season there may be lambs, calves, kids and piglets on
the farm.

Children can touch, stroke and feed the animals and help
with mucking out, or just look around. There are gardening
activities and a summer play-scheme during the six weeks'
holiday.

Educational provision
Worksheets will be available for teachers.

Disabled
Toilets and hard paths all the way round. There is riding for
the disabled at weekends (providing it is arranged through the
Camden Gateway Club or Camden Association for the
Disabled), and gardening activities.

KENWOOD HOUSE

(See Iveagh Bequest.)

KEW BRIDGE ENGINES TRUST

The Pumping Station, Kew Bridge Road, Brentford, London W4
Tel: 01-568 4757

Underground: Gunnersbury
British Rail: Kew Bridge

Open
11 a.m. – 5 p.m. Sat, Sun and Bank holiday Mon.
Closed Mon to Fri and Christmas weekend.

Admission charges
Children   70p.
Adults   £1.20.
Family   (2 adults and 2/3 children) £3.50. 10% reduction
on 12 or more.

Kew Bridge Engines Trust has eight steam-powered pumping
engines, five of which are now working-under steam. They
were used to pump water both for London and to drain
Cornish tin and copper mines. The 90-inch engine is now the
largest beam engine in steam in the world, its beam weighing
35 tons and delivering 472 gallons per stroke. From the beam
gallery visitors can marvel at the size, smooth operation and
the elegance of this engine under steam. The museum also has
a forge, a Victorian workshop and relics of London's water
supply system, and a small display of models illustrates steam
engine types.

Educational provision
A volunteer guide is sometimes available for school parties.

Refreshments
Cafeteria open during museum hours.

Shop
Shop open during museum hours sells books, postcards and
souvenirs.

Disabled

The disabled have access to the car park and the ground floor of the museum. There are special toilets available.

KEW GARDENS

**Royal Botanic Gardens, Kew, Richmond,
Surrey TW9 3AB
Tel: 01-940 1171**

Underground: Kew Gardens
British Rail: Kew Gardens or Kew Bridge

Open

10 a.m. – 8 p.m. or dusk if earlier Daily.
Closed Christmas Day and New Year's Day.

Admission charges

Children (under 10) free.
Adults 15p.
School Parties
Admitted free except on Sat, Sun and Public holidays.
(Over 10s must obtain voucher at least 7 days beforehand).
Note: no dogs except guide dogs.

Kew Gardens covers 300 acres and has a wide range of plants from all over the world, some in glasshouses. Plants are from the desert, the tropical rainforest, and there are alpines in the new Alpine House. The lake has ducks and geese and lakeside plants. The museum with exhibits on useful plants includes tea, cocoa, medicinal plants, poisons (for arrows) and rubber trees. The Wood museum has samples of British timbers with wooden objects and models. The Marianne North gallery has 832 paintings of plants and flowers with scenes from various countries.

Educational provision

Two guide lecturers are available to take parties of not more than 25 people, Mon to Fri (except Public holidays).

Applications for these must be at least 2 weeks in advance and 6 weeks in summer. Quiz sheets are also available.

Refreshments
Refreshment Pavilion and tea bar open in the summer.
Tea bar open in winter from 12 noon – 3 p.m.

Shop
Shop open from 10 a.m. – 5.50 p.m. sells books of horticultural and botanical interest, guides, maps, postcards, slides, souvenirs and gifts.

Disabled
There is level access throughout the gardens, and access is also available to the glasshouses and museums. Wheelchairs may be hired for 15p for as long as required from the Main Gate.

KEW PALACE

Kew Gardens, Kew, Surrey
Tel: 01-940 3321

Underground: Kew Gardens
British Rail: Kew Bridge

Open
Apr – Sept   11 a.m. – 5.30 p.m. Daily.
Closed Oct to Mar.

Admission charges
Children   30p.
Adults   60p.
OAP   30p.
Parties of 11 or more   10% discount.
School Parties
Free if booked 14 days in advance.

Kew Palace was known originally as 'The Dutch House' and is the smallest and most intimate of Royal Palaces. It was built in 1631 by Samuel Fortey, a London merchant of Dutch parentage, in the low countries' renaissance style. The four-storey house was acquired on lease by George II for Queen Caroline about 1730. It was later occupied by Frederick, Prince of Wales, and after his death by his widow whose son George III purchased it in 1781 as a nursery for the numerous Royal children. Their mother Queen Charlotte died there in 1818. Many alterations, especially internally, were carried out by Prince Frederick between 1737 and 1748, probably under the supervision of William Kent, and some of the furniture now in the building dates back to this time. The Queens' drawing room is set for a musical evening while a King's fishing tackle, children's play things, and other bygones vividly evoke the Royal occupants.

Educational provision
Free information sheet available.

Refreshments
Cafeteria available as for Kew Gardens.

Shop
Shop open during visiting hours sells illustrated guide books, colour postcards and 35mm colour slides.

KINGSBURY WATERMILL MUSEUM

St Michael's Street, St Albans, Herts AL3 4SJ
Tel: 0727 53502

British Rail: St Albans

Open
Summer   10.30 a.m. – 6 p.m. Tues to Sat;
12 noon – 6 p.m. Sun.
Winter   11 a.m. – 5 p.m. Tues to Sat; 12 noon – 5 p.m. Sun.
Closed Mon.

Admission charges
Children   25p.
Adults   50p.
Student   35p.

Kingsbury Watermill Museum is a working watermill with a working wheel and a collection of farm and dairy and country-living artefacts. There is also an Art Gallery. Visiting parties should make prior arrangements and avoid weekends.

Educational provision
A guide book is available with details of the history and workings of the Watermill.

Refreshments
Cafeteria open during museum hours.

Shop
Shop open during museum hours sells gifts and pottery.

Disabled
No facilities for the disabled.

KINGSTON HERITAGE CENTRE

Fairfield West, Kingston-Upon-Thames, Surrey KT1 2PS
Tel: 01-546 5386

British Rail: Kingston

Open
10 a.m. – 5 p.m. Mon to Sat.
Closed Sun.

Admission charges
Free.

The **Kingston Heritage Centre** has both temporary and permanent exhibitions. The permanent exhibitions include local history where archaeological finds with articles from medieval times such as pottery, seals, pilgrim badges and weapons are displayed.

There is a permanent exhibition devoted to Edward Muybridge (1830-1904), the pioneer of motion photography and photographer of movement. It includes a replica of his famous invention, the zoopraxiscope, the first ever projector of moving pictures. A video film shows the image which the zoopraxiscope projects and an audio-visual film demonstrates how Muybridge photographed moving subjects, especially horses.

The third permanent exhibition is a made-in-Kingston section, which deals with the more recent developments in trade and industry in Kingston.

Educational provision

There is a schools' loan scheme under which artefacts from the museum are sent out to schools. Guided tours for school parties are also available.

Shop

Shop open during visiting hours sells books, postcards and souvenirs.

Disabled

The main exhibition areas are on the ground floor and accessible to the disabled.

KNOLE (National Trust)

Sevenoaks, Kent TN15 0RP
Tel: (Sevenoaks) 0732 450608

British Rail: Sevenoaks

Open

Apr – Oct 11 a.m. – 5 p.m. Wed to Sat and Bank holiday Mon; 2 – 5 p.m. Sun (last admissions one hour before closing). Closed Nov to Mar and Mon and Tues.
Tues open to pre-booked guided parties except when following a Bank holiday Mon.

Admission charges

Children £1.   Fri £2.50
Adults £2.   Fri £2.50.
Party rates
(except Tues or Fri) if pre-booked and minimum 25 persons

Children   80p.
Adults   £1.50.
Gardens
Children   25p.
Adults   50p.

Knole was built in the mid 15th century originally as an archipiscopal palace. It passed through the ownership of Henry VIII, Elizabeth I and the Sackville family to the National Trust who now own it. It is one of the largest private houses in England to be opened to the public, who have been visiting it for two to three centuries. It contains many pictures and one of the most important collections in the world of 17th century English upholstered furniture. Friday is connoisseurs' day when extra rooms may be shown. The gardens are open on the first Wednesday in each month from May to September.

Educational provision
Advice and help given to teachers and free guide book available.

Shop
Shop open during visiting hours sells postcards, books, guides, souvenirs and colouring charts.

LASERIUM
(See London Planetarium.)

LEE VALLEY PARK
(See Hayes Hill Farm.)

LEIGHTON HOUSE

12 Holland Park Road, London W14
Tel: 01-602 3316

Underground: High Street Kensington

Open
11 a.m. – 5 p.m. Mon to Sat.
Closed Sun and Bank holidays.

Admission charges
Free.

Leighton House is a Victorian purpose-built artist's studio house. It is decorated with period paper and fabrics. Furniture from the Victoria and Albert Museum gives an impression of how the house looked in its heyday. The 'Arab' Hall was constructed to house Leighton's collection of Syrian and Islamic tiles and this recreation of the orient is more lavish and mysterious than anything ever seen in Damascus or Cairo – a piece of quintessential Victoriana and quite unique. The house contains a collection of paintings and drawings by Leighton and a number of works on loan from the Tate Gallery including works by Burne-Jones, Millais, and other Victorian contemporaries. The house is particularly valuable as a home as well as a gallery. In it Lord Leighton lived, worked and entertained with all the lavish domestic service which the Victorians took so completely for granted. As a working artist's home it contrasts well with the more formal and grand Linley Sambourne House and visits to both houses can be arranged in conjunction with lectures and work programmes.

Educational provision
A guided tour of the house and slide lectures are available, also in conjunction with a tour of Linley Sambourne House. Help can be given to the organising teacher in preparing worksheets. There are also tours with lectures on the Houses, design or architecture, for advanced students.

LINLEY SAMBOURNE HOUSE

18 Stafford Terrace, Kensington, London W8 7BH
Tel: 01-994 1019 or 622 6360

Underground: Kensington High Street

Open
Mar – Oct   10 a.m. – 4 p.m. Wed; 2 – 5 p.m. Sun.
Other times by arrangement for groups of 15 or more.
Closed Mon, Tues, Thurs, Fri, Sat and Nov to Feb.

Admission charges
£1.50 per person. £1.35 per person for groups of 15 or more.

Linley Sambourne House is a late 19th century home which has survived intact with its original furnishing and decorations. Sambourne, an artist on Punch magazine, decorated the house in the artistic style of the period. There are many works by Sambourne and his contemporaries, but the chief interest of the house is as an authentic survival rather than a recreation of the Victorian period. The overall picture and atmosphere of a middle class home of the 1880s is unique.

Educational provision
The house is of particular interest to students of the decorative arts and interior design, as well as, possibly, 'A' Level History students. The House is only suitable for students over 16 years of age, and not suitable for younger children in groups, though they are welcome with parents.

Shop
Shop open during the same times as the House sells postcards, guidebooks, various other books and small objects of special interest to those studying the Victorian period.

LIVERY COMPANY HALLS OF THE CITY OF LONDON

City of London Information Bureau, St Paul's Churchyard, London EC4
Tel: 01-606 3030

Open
About twice a year depending on the Livery Hall. Open days obtainable from the address above. Guided tours only.

Admission charges
Free.

There are about 20 **Livery Company Halls** such as that of the Goldsmiths or Apothecaries which are open to the public on several days each year. For details contact the above address.

LIVESEY MUSEUM

682 Old Kent Road, London SE15 1JF
Tel: 01-639 5604

Underground: Elephant and Castle (2 miles – bus needed)

Open
10 a.m. – 5 p.m. Mon to Sat.
Closed Sun and days when there is no exhibition held.

Admission charges
Free.

The **Livesey Museum** was reopened after being bombed in the Second World War, in 1974, as a gallery for temporary exhibitions. The museum lacks a permanent collection but has 'street furniture' including a toll gate on display in the museum courtyard. The aim of the museum is to provide the general public, and especially the local community with a succession of changing exhibitions. Many deal with the local history of Southwark.

Special events
For details of future events, phone the Museum.

Educational provision
Each exhibition has its own specially designed education programme including slide-talk, activities, worksheets and hand-outs – all available free. The museum staff particularly welcome group visits (which can vary from 1 to 2 hours) and, being a small museum, can offer a friendly and personal service.

Shop
Shop open during museum hours sells pens, pencils, postcards, and items relating to the current exhibition topic.

LONDON AIRPORT

(See Heathrow Airport.)

LONDON BRASS RUBBING CENTRE

**St James' Church, Piccadilly, London W1
Tel: 01-437 6023**

Underground: Piccadilly Circus and Green Park

Open
10 a.m. – 6 p.m. Mon to Sat; 12 noon – 6 p.m. Sun.
Closed Christmas Day.

Admission charges
Fees for brass rubbing start at 50p.

The **London Brass Rubbing Centre** has a collection of about seventy facsimiles of some of the most famous Medieval and Tudor brasses from English parish churches. They are all accurate pictures of the past, telling us about social customs, dress, armour, trades, professions, family stories, depicting a 350 year period of this country's history. Many of them have inscriptions telling us more about the people they commemorate.

Visitors may make their own brass rubbings of any of the brasses in the exhibition. Materials and instruction are provided. It is a surprisingly easy technique which needs no artistic skill.

Educational provision
Booklet of historical notes to the brasses available.

Shop
Shop sells ready-made rubbings, books, models, plaques and historical artefacts.

Disabled
Entrance is down an iron staircase but groups from special schools for the handicapped are welcome.

LONDON BUTTERFLY HOUSE

Syon Park, Brentford, Middlesex
Tel: 01-560 7272

Underground: Gunnersbury
British Rail: Kew Bridge and Isleworth

Open
Feb 15 – Oct 31 10 a.m. – 5 p.m. Daily.
Nov 1 – Feb 14 10 a.m. – 3.30 p.m. Daily.
Closed Christmas Eve, Christmas Day and Boxing Day.

Admission charges

Children £1.
Adults £1.80.
OAP £1.20.
Family ticket
parents and 2-4 children £5.

The **London Butterfly House** has tropical greenhouse gardens where visitors can stroll among free-flying butterflies from all over the world. It is the first butterfly 'safari park' in Europe. All stages of breeding, including egg-laying, caterpillar rearing and courtship displays among the tropical flowers may be closely observed and photographed. There is a separate section devoted to educational and pictorial displays as well as an exhibition of other fascinating live insects like giant spiders, leaf-cutting ants, stick insects and locusts.

Refreshments
Cafeteria in Syon Park.

Shop
Shop open during visiting hours sells books, T-shirts, butterfly jigsaws, insect tags and ornaments, mounted butterflies and souvenirs.

Disabled
Access for wheelchairs.

LONDON CAB COMPANY MUSEUM

1-3 Brixton Road, London SW9 6DJ
Tel: 01-735 3705

Underground: Oval

Open
9 a.m. – 5 p.m. Mon to Fri; 9 a.m. – 2 p.m. Sat.
Closed weekends and Bank holidays.

Admission charges
Free.

The **London Cab Company Museum** has vehicles ranging from 1907 to the present day. The Unic, made in 1907, had a French-made engine and English chassis, with an English body and is one of the earliest examples of a non-horse pulled motor taxi. There are several Beardmores, from the 1932 high-lot (motor above chassis rather than underslung) to a couple made in the 1960s which have alloy and fibre-glass panelled bodies on a timber frame. The FX is one of the earliest diesel taxis with three doors – including open access to a luggage compartment at the side. There are two prototypes – a Lucas electric taxi exhibited at the Motor Show in the 1970s but not yet adopted and a Metro made in 1969 by Metro-Cammell with an unusual combination of fibre-glass body and diesel engine.

Refreshments
Vending machines serve drinks and confectionery.

Disabled
A ramp leads to the front entrance and disabled visitors are allowed through the workshops to the museum entrance.

LONDON CENTRAL MOSQUE

146 Park Road, London NW8 7RG
Tel: None.

Underground: Baker Street

Open
10 a.m. – 4 p.m. Daily.
Never closed.

Admission charges
Free.

The **London Central Mosque** was built in the 1970s after an international competition to select the most appropriate building had been won by Sir Frederick Gibberd, a distinguished British architect. The design has four elements: two prayer halls, a three-storey building which includes administrative offices, a residential block, and the minaret.

The main prayer hall has a very large metal and concrete dome clad on the outside with copper alloy giving it a very distinctive gold appearance. On the inside it has a circular frieze of gold and turqoise tiles in traditional patterns. The Mosque is an integral part of the Islamic Cultural Centre where classes are held in Arabic and in Islamic religious knowledge. Lectures on Islam can be given to visiting parties.

Educational provision
Lecture room available.

Shop
Shop open from 9.30 a.m. – 5 p.m. sells books on Islam.

LONDON DIAMOND CENTRE

10 Hanover Street, London WR1 9HF
Tel: 01-629 5511

Underground: Oxford Circus

Open
9.30 a.m. – 5.30 p.m. Mon to Fri; 9.30 a.m. – 1.30 p.m. Sat. Closed Sun.

Admission charges
Children £2.45.
Adults £2.45.
School Parties
£2.45 per person.

The **London Diamond Centre's** guided tours show visitors the processes of diamond mining, cutting and polishing. A 5-minute video shows mining and sorting of raw diamonds of which only some 25% are suitable quality for jewellery, the rest being used for industrial purposes. Polishing, cleaning, shaping and facetting are explained – the finished gemstone has 58 facets. The upstairs showroom displays the finished product from semi-precious agates to diamonds, both loose and mounted.

Educational provision
Worksheets are available on request.

LONDON DUNGEON

28-34 Tooley Street, London SE1 2SZ
Tel: 01-403 0606

Underground: London Bridge

Open
Apr – Sept   10 a.m. – 5.45 p.m. Daily.
Oct – Mar   10 a.m. – 4.30 p.m. Daily.
Never closed.

Admission charges
Children (under 14) £2.
Adults £3.50.
School Parties
(10 or more) 10% discount; (20 or more) £1.50 per person plus one free ticket.

The **London Dungeon** is the world's first fantasy exhibition of British Medieval History with life-size scenes depicting Medieval Legends, the Dark Ages, the Reformation, the Tortures of the Tower, Demonology, Astrology and Witchcraft.

The *Times* Educational Supplement said of it 'A detailed and serious look at the horrors of murder and torture so realistically illustrated, with plenty of bloody figures, they impress far more than any array of mere objects could ever do'.

Educational provision

Questionnaires in English, French or German are provided free to school parties. Project suggestions are also available. The Trial and Tribulation Centre, available free, is an education centre and packed lunches may be eaten here.

Refreshments

Cafeteria open during visiting hours.

Shop

Souvenir counter open during visiting hours.

LONDON FIRE BRIGADE MUSEUM

94A Southwark Bridge Road, London SE1
Tel: 01-587 4273
Messages can be left on 01-587 4066

Underground: Borough
British Rail: Waterloo and London Bridge

Open

10 a.m. – 4 p.m. Mon to Fri by appointment only.
Closed Sat, Sun and Public holidays.

Admission charges

Free. (Children must be over 10 and parties less than 12 in number and pre-booked).

The **London Fire Brigade Museum** has fire-fighting memorabilia dating back to the 17th century including vehicles, equipment, uniforms and medals. Three rooms are furnished as in the time of the first chief officer in the 19th century and the Braidwood Room – in memory of a chief officer killed in mid-19th century – has insurance company fire marks, leather buckets, fire grenades and a portion of 16th century water main.

The Massey-Shaw Room has personal effects, a medal collection and photographs of Victorian appliances. Modern appliances are on the landing. At the top of the museum is the War Room with paintings and sketches and two unexploded bombs (which have been defused). The International Room has badges, pennons, uniforms and helmets from fire brigades throughout the world.

LONDON LIVING STEAM MUSEUM

(See Kew Bridge Engines Trust.)

LONDON PLANETARIUM

Marylebone Road, London NW1 5LR
Tel: 01-486 1121

Underground: Baker Street

Open
11 a.m. – 4.30 p.m. Daily.
Closed Christmas Day.

Admission charges
Children £1.20.
Adults £1.85.
School Parties
£1.

The **London Planetarium's** general programme unveils some of the mysteries of the universe with stunning visual effects. Under the green copper dome visitors can take an exciting journey into the universe of stars and planets, comets and galaxies. This man-made universe is produced by a massive, complex star projector weighing over two tons and containing some 29,000 separate parts. It can transport the viewer back and forward in time and space, and, with additional special effects will create an unforgettable experience. Visits include free admission to the Astronomers' Gallery, depicting some great astronomers of the past.

Laser light concerts are given most evenings in the Planetarium. For details phone 01-486 2242.

Educational provision
School programme given during term time Tues to Fri at 11 a.m. and Wed at 1 p.m. Free teachers' pack with every advance booking – contains teachers' notes, worksheets and sources of astronomical material.

Refreshments
Cafeteria open 10 a.m. – 5.30 p.m.

Shop
Shop sells posters, books and souvenir guide for the Planetarium.

LONDON SCHOOLS' PLANETARIUM

Wandsworth School, Sutherland Grove, London SW18
Tel: 01-788 4253

Underground: Southfields

Open
During term time 9.30 a.m. – 4.30 p.m. Mon to Fri. Schools should book a half term in advance.
Closed school holidays.

Admission charges
Free. The Planetarium is only open to school parties and adult education establishments.

The **London Schools' Planetarium** has courses from primary to 'A' level. Typical introductory courses for schools cover:

eclipses, birth of stars, the rotating earth, risings and settings, the need for a calendar, the planets and the galaxies, and many more topics.

For primary schools there are courses on elementary astronomy and the night sky. At secondary level there are introductory courses and exam-related courses: CSE Environmental Science, 'O' and 'A' Level Physics and 'A' Level English – Chaucer's Skies.

Educational provision
Lecture rooms, teachers' guides and worksheets are all available and there are inservice courses embodying demonstrations and discussions, on techniques and subject matter, visual aids, resource material and school project work.

Shop
Shop open during visiting hours sells astronomical postcards and wall charts.

Disabled
There is flat access for wheelchairs.

LONDON TOY AND MODEL MUSEUM

23 Craven Hill, London W2 3EN
Tel: 01-262 7905

Underground: Lancaster Gate
British Rail: Paddington

Open
10 a.m. – 5.30 p.m. Tues to Sat; 11 a.m. – 5 p.m. Sun.
Closed Mon except Bank holidays, Christmas Day,
New Year's Day.

Admission charges
Children (over 5) 60p.
Adults £1.80.
OAP, Student £1.20.

School Parties and Groups
Children 40p.
Adults £1.20.

The **London Toy and Model Museum** is one of the world's great independent family museums. On display are superb examples of model and toy trains, tin toys, toy fire engines, toy animals, and a small but representative collection of dolls. The Tiatsa miniature vehicle collection in Gallery 7 contains 15,000 items which are on revolving exhibition here with 2,000 on view at any time. This includes famous names such as Dinky, Corgi, Lesney and Solido.

Visitors can ride on a steam train, play on the playbus, and attempt take-off procedures on a Comet 4B flight simulator.

Educational provision
Worksheets and quizzes can be provided and special talks by prior arrangement for school visits.

Refreshments
Cafeteria open in normal museum hours sells light snacks suitable for all ages.

Shop
Shop open during museum hours sells juvenalia, books on toys and models and gift items from 15p to £50.

Disabled
There are ramps to the upper gallery and gardens for the disabled.

LONDON TRANSPORT MUSEUM

Covent Garden, London WC2E 7BB
Tel: 01-379 6344

Underground: Covent Garden, Charing Cross or Leicester Square

---

Open

10 a.m. – 6 p.m. (last admission 5.15 p.m.) Daily.
Closed Christmas Day and Boxing Day.

Admission charges

Children (5-16) £1.
Adults £2.20.
OAP, UB40 and *Student* £1.
School Parties
Child 80p and one teacher ticket per 8 pupils
Family ticket for 2 adults and any 2 of the reduced price
category for £5 (saving £1.40).

The **London Transport Museum** has buses, motorbuses,
trams, trolleybuses, underground trains, video displays,
models, photographs and posters, illustrating the fascinating
story of the development of London's Transport systems and
their impact on the way people live and work in the capital.
Visitors can 'drive' a bus, a tram and a train and there are a
number of unique working exhibits such as a full-size section
of tube tunnel with a set of points and signals to operate. The
'dead man's handle' of a tube train is a favourite working
exhibit. Children love the colour and strange shapes of the old
horse buses and train lovers will find a steam locomotive used
on the world's first underground railway.

There are film shows or other activities every weekend, and
during half term and Bank holiday weekends.

Educational provision

A full education service is available for parties from schools
and colleges. Worksheets are in three sorts: a 2-colour version
with cut-out models for 8-13 year olds, simpler version for 6-8
years and very simple version for under 6s.

Refreshments

Coffee shop open 11 a.m. – 5 p.m.

Shop

Shop open 10 a.m. – 5.45 p.m. selling postcards, posters, books
and attractive and unusual souvenirs.

Disabled
Registered handicapped visitors are admitted free. Toilets and access to almost every part of the museum, including coffee shop and lecture hall.

LONDON WATERBUS COMPANY

Camden Lock, London NW1 8AF
Tel: 01-482 2550

Underground: Camden Town (for Camden Lock) or
            Warwick Avenue (for Little Venice)

Open
Oct – Apr the service runs on weekends only.
Apr – Oct (summer season) the service runs daily with departures every hour on the hour.

Admission charges
Children from 40p to £2.
Adults from 60p to £3.85
OAP from 40p to £2.
The higher prices include discounted London Zoo entrance.
School Parties
Two teachers free with each group of 20 children if pre-booked.

The **London Waterbus** runs between Camden Lock and Little Venice via London Zoo. Little Venice forms the junction of the Regent's Canal and the Grand Union Canal. In the centre of the pool is the small and attractive Browning's Island where the poet lived. The canal then goes through the 272-yard long Maida Hill Tunnel and into the beautiful Regents Park, where it is in a leafy cutting on the fringe of the park – there is no finer stretch of urban waterway in the country. Then on to the London Zoo where the Company has its own landing stage. After the Zoo the greenery of Regents Park gives way to elegant houses with colourful gardens

146

backing on the water. Finally the canal reaches Camden Lock with its graceful iron moving bridge and double lock gates, and delightful collection of craft workshops and studios set in the converted stables and warehouses around terraced gardens.

Educational provision
Full briefing sheets are available for teachers – please ask in advance or when booking.

Disabled
The boats can accommodate a limited number of wheelchair-bound passengers – please phone beforehand. Access is over cobbles to paved area or via tow-path (paved and without steps).

LONDON ZOO

Regent's Park, London NW1 4RY
Tel: 01-722 3333

Underground: Camden Town
British Rail: Marylebone and Euston

Open
Summer 9 a.m. – 6 p.m. or dusk (7 on Sun) Daily.
Winter 10 a.m. – dusk Daily.
Closed Christmas Day.

Admission charges
Mar 1 – Nov 30
Children (5-16) £1.60.
Adults £3.20.
OAP £1.25.
Student £2.35.
Party Rates
Schools (20+) Youth Groups (6+)
Children (5-16) £1.25.
Adults £2.50.
Charges from Nov 30, 1985 are not available at time of going to print.

The **London Zoo**, planned and developed by Sir Hugh Casson, has over 8,000 animals, including the rare Giant Pandas, Great Apes, a fine collection of nocturnal animals in the moonlight world, birds, reptiles, amphibians, fishes and insects. Feed times are: sealions 12 noon and 3 p.m. (except Fridays). Reptiles 2.30 p.m. (Fridays only), pelicans 2.45 p.m., polar bears 3 p.m. (most days), birds of prey 3.15 p.m. Cows are milked in the Children's Zoo daily at 3 p.m. On fine days from Easter to the end of September there are camel, pony, donkey and llama trap rides. The world-famous aviary was designed by Lord Snowdon.

1985 sees a special promotion of the Ungulates section (hoofed animals).

Educational provision
The Zoo has tours for all ages and abilities and talks ranging from 'Touching and Learning' and 'Nasty Animals' through to 'A' level studies. Quiz sheets are part of some of these courses. Enquiries to the Zoo number, extension 111.

Refreshments
Cafeteria in the Zoo is open throughout the year, and other cafes and kiosks throughout the summer months. Restaurant is open from 10 a.m. – half-hour before closing time and serves children's meals. School packed lunches may be eaten in the front half of the Regent's cafeteria.

Shop
Shop open 9.30 a.m. – 4.45 p.m. (summer) and 10 a.m. – 3.45 p.m. (winter), sells toys, books, postcards, films and souvenirs. Extra camera shop open during the summer months.

Disabled
Special ramps into some houses and the cafe in the Zoo, also toilet facilities.

LORDS CRICKET MUSEUM
(See Cricket Museum.)

LULLINGSTONE ROMAN VILLA

Lullingstone, near Dartford, Kent
Tel: 0322 863467

British Rail: Eynsford

Open
Mar 15 – Oct 15 9.30 a.m. – 6.30 p.m. Mon to Sat;
2 – 6.30 p.m. Sun (all day Sun Apr 1 – Sept 30).
Oct 16 – Mar 14 9.30 a.m. – 6.30 p.m. Mon to Sat;
2 – 4 p.m. Sun.
Closed Christmas Eve, Christmas Day, Boxing Day,
New Year's Day.

Admission charges
Summer
Children 50p.
Adults 90p.
Winter
Children 25p.
Adults 50p.
Party voucher
For 11 or more 10% off.
School Parties
Free entry if form is applied for.

Lullingstone Roman Villa still has original flint walls and also
two mosaic floors – one of Pegasus the Winged Horse with a
border which originally depicted the four seasons, three of
which now remain. The other mosaic shows the Abduction of
Europa by Jupiter in the Guise of a Bull, and this has a Latin
inscription. Pottery on show features Samian ware, Nene
Valley ware and black metallic beakers from the Rhineland.
There are animal skeletons and a man and a baby all of them
dating from Roman times.

Shop
Shop open same hours as monument selling postcards, guide
book, souvenirs and various books.

Disabled

At present the disabled can see all the exhibits on the ground floor and there are plans for extending the provision.

LYRIC THEATRE, HAMMERSMITH

King Street, London W6 0QL
Tel: 01-741 0824

Underground: Hammersmith

Open

10 a.m. – 8 p.m. Mon to Sat. Tours by arrangement.
Closed Sun and some Bank holidays.

Charges for tours

Children   25p in groups up to 12.
Adults   25p in groups up to 12.
School Parties
25p per head.

The **Lyric Theatre** tour takes visitors backstage, round the studio theatre and the main auditorium.

Apart from the tour, the theatre holds regular exhibitions of artists' works, and has a craft fair most Saturdays.

Educational provision

Information sheets are provided for the tour and worksheets for primary pupils.

Refreshments

Restaurant in the main foyer open 10 a.m. – 8 p.m., will serve children's meals by arrangement.

Disabled

Access by lift from street level and toilet facilities.

MADAME TUSSAUD'S

Marylebone Road, London NW1 5LR
Tel: 01-935 6861

Underground: Baker Street

Open
Oct – Mar   10 a.m. – 5.30 p.m. Daily
Apr – Sept   10 a.m. – 6 p.m. Daily.
Closed Christmas Day.

Admission charges
Children   £1.85
Adults   £3.30.
School Parties
Children under 16 £1.65 (joint ticket with planetarium £2.25).

Madame Tussaud's famous models in wax depict historical tableaux, sportsmen, pop stars, kings, queens, and the present Royal family. Here are heads of state, past and present. The chamber of horrors and the battle of Trafalgar displays include sound, light and special effects. If possible, it is best to visit outside August.

Educational provision
Worksheets and free guidebooks available from the party booking office.

Refreshments
Cafeteria open 10 a.m. – 5.30 p.m.

Shop
Shop open 10 a.m. – 5.30 p.m. selling guidebooks, postcards, keyrings, badges, rubbers, pencils, pens, brooches and souvenirs.

Disabled
Facilities can be arranged if prior notice of visit is given to the Duty Manager.

151

MANRESA HOUSE, MOUNT CLARE AND DOWNSHIRE HOUSE

Garnett College, Holybourne Avenue, Roehampton, London SW15 4 JD
Tel: 01-789 6688
(ask for Michael Bampton, the Conservator)

Underground: East Putney or Putney Bridge
British Rail: Putney

Open
By arrangement – parties (ideally about 15 in number) or individuals welcome, Sat afternoon the best time.

Admission charges
Free.

Manresa House, Mount Clare and **Downshire House** are all used by Garnett College of Education. The tour usually starts with Downshire House with its beautiful setting, and continues to Manresa House. This House stands in 12 acres of grounds overlooking Richmond Park. It was designed in the early 1760s by Sir William Chambers, the architect of Somerset House, as a country villa for the second Earl of Bessborough. It has a fine Ionic portico with curved staircase down to the park. Mount Clare, the third house, is a finely appointed 18th century house built in 1772 for George Clive, a cousin of Lord Clive. The architect was almost certainly Robert Taylor. Extensive redecoration some 10 years later was done by Placido Columbani for Sir John Dick. Its fine ceilings and marble plaques are by Shubin. The Conservator gives a guided tour which is enthusiastic and informative.

Educational provision
Plenty of lecture rooms available and short notes on the houses.

Refreshments
If pre-booked teas (and lunches sometimes) can be provided at very reasonable cost.

Disabled
Manresa House has toilets, lift and ramps by arrangement, and all important parts of the house are accessible. Mount Clare also has toilets but not so accessible – there are a few steps to the ground floor.

MANSION HOUSE

Bank, London EC4N 8BH
Tel: 01-626 2500

Underground: Bank

Open
Mid Sept – 31 July   Organised tours of parties of about 30 only at 11 a.m. and 2 p.m. Tues, Wed and Thurs.
Closed 1 Aug to mid-Sept, Fri to Mon, Bank holiday periods and when used for functions.

Admission charges
Free. (Not suitable for children under the age of 12).

The **Mansion House** was designed by George Dance and built in the mid-18th century. Major functions are held in the Egyptian Hall where 23 carat gold leaf has been used as decoration. The Hall has Corinthian columns and a barrel ceiling, a true Palladian design in pale blue and ivory. The sumptuous Venetian Parlour has enriched plasterwork on the ceiling, a specially designed carpet made in 1976, and contains furniture by Hepplewhite. Also open to the public are the State Drawing Room, The Justice Room and the Saloon. Fine examples of skilled plasterwork which have been carefully preserved can be found throughout the house.

The Plate Room contains cases of gold plate presented by former Lord Mayors and to Lord Mayors when travelling abroad. Two famous pieces are the State of the Queen mounted on the charger Winston, and the rigged model of the

Great Harry – the first ship of the Royal Navy which was built in Kent in 1516.

Disabled
Lift to the first floor. The House can take up to 6 wheelchair visitors at a time.

MARBLE HILL HOUSE

Richmond Road, Twickenham, Middlesex TW1 2NL
Tel: 01-892 5115

British Rail: St Margaret's

Open
Feb – Oct   10 a.m. – 5 p.m. Sat to Thurs.
Nov – Jan   10 a.m. – 4 p.m. Sat to Thurs.
Closed Fri, Christmas Eve and Christmas Day.

Admission charges
Free.

Marble Hill House was built in 1724-9 as a summer villa for Henrietta Howard, later Countess of Suffolk. It is a perfect Palladian villa situated by the Thames, based on a drawing by the architect, Colin Campbell, but much influenced by Lord Herbert, the future Earl of Pembroke. Marble Hill was restored by the GLC and opened in 1966. It has since been stocked with paintings of Lady Suffolk's period including an early Reynolds portrait and Richard Wilson's charming view of the Thames at Marble Hill. Furniture includes the Northey Suite with its fine original needlework.

Educational provision
Introductions to the house can be made by appointment.
(Ms Gene Adams, ILEA Centre of Learning Resources
tel: 01-633 2751/2).

154

Refreshments
Light refreshments available in the Stable Block Cafe from
April to September.

Shop
Sales desk open during visiting hours sells guides and
postcards.

Disabled
Toilets and ground floor access.

MARITIME TRUST MUSEUM

(See Historic Ship Collection.)

MARLBOROUGH HOUSE

Pall Mall, London SW1
Tel: 01-930 9249

Underground: Green Park

Open
By appointment only. Conducted tours of the house at 11 a.m.
and 3 p.m. Mon to Fri.
Closed Sat and Sun and for functions.

Admission charges
50p per person.

Marlborough House is a royal palace now used as a
Commonwealth conference centre. It was built by Wren in
1709-11 and the ground floor state rooms are open to the
public, when not used for functions. The Blenheim room has
wall paintings of the Battle of Blenheim and a ceiling by
Gentileschi. On the staircases are wall paintings by Laguerre
of battle scenes, including Blenheim and Ramilies.

Educational provision
An educational booklet on Marlborough House is available –
cost 70p.

MAUGHAN COLLECTION OF
THEATRICAL PAINTING
(See National Theatre.)

MILL CHURCH, REIGATE
Reigate Heath, Flanchford Road, Reigate, Surrey

British Rail: Reigate

Open
8.30 a.m. – 4 p.m. Daily.
Closed Christmas Day.

Admission charges
Free.

The **Mill Church, Reigate** attracts visitors from all over the
world. Until about 1859 it was a working windmill but had to
close for economic reasons – it took four horses to drag the
wagons to this mill along the muddy tracks where other local
mills used only two horses. It was taken over by the Church in
1880 and consecrated in 1884. Although most of the workings
have been removed for safety reasons, it still retains the look of
the former mill. The roundel – base – is of brick and the main
structure is clad in timber weatherboarding. It still has the
original wooden sails. The church stands on the heath and is
much sketched in summer. It is close to the golf clubhouse and
if it is locked during the above hours, a key can be obtained
from the manager of the golf club.

There is a church service at 3 p.m. every third Sunday in the
month from May to October.

MILTON'S COTTAGE

Deanway, Chalfont St Giles, Bucks
Tel: (Chalfont) 02407 2313

British Rail: Amersham

Open
Feb – Oct   10 a.m. – 1 p.m. and 2 – 6 p.m. Tues to Sat;
2 – 6 p.m. Sun.
Closed Nov to Jan.

Admission charges
Children   30p.
Adults   80p.
School Parties
over 20, 60p each.

This is **Milton's 16th century cottage** with two rooms open to
the public. The kitchen has original fireplaces and many relics
of Bucks and Chalfont St Giles. Milton's study contains 93
rare books including first editions of *Paradise Lost* and
Paradise Regained. Also, there is a large collection of Milton's
works in translation including Japanese and Chinese editions.
The cottage is surrounded by one acre of charming cottage
garden.

MONUMENT

Monument Street, London EC3R 8AH
Tel: 01-626 2717

Underground: Monument

Open
Apr – Sept   9 a.m. – 6 p.m. Mon to Sat; 2 – 6 p.m. Sun.
Oct – Mar   9 a.m. – 4 p.m. Mon to Sat.
Closed Sun from Oct to Mar.

Admission charges
Children 25p.
Adults 50p.

The **Monument** was completed in 1677 to commemorate the Great Fire of London which took place in 1666. It is a column made of Portland Stone and standing 202 feet high (202 feet being the distance from the spot in Pudding Lane where the Great Fire was alleged to have started). A spiral staircase of 311 steps leads to the public gallery which is at a height of 160 feet and from which visitors have a magnificent view across London.

Special events
On the second Saturday in November annually, the Lord Mayor's show passes.

MOSQUITO AIRCRAFT MUSEUM

Salisbury Hall, PO Box 107, London Colney, Herts
Tel: (Bowmansgreen) 0727 22051

British Rail: Barnet

Open
Easter – end of Oct 10.30 a.m. – 5.30 p.m. Sun, Bank holiday Mon.
July, Aug, Sept 2 – 5.30 p.m. Thurs.
Also open by appointment at other times.
Closed Nov to Easter.

Admission charges
Children 25p.
Adults 75p.

The **Mosquito Aircraft Museum** is a unique collection of planes and photographs. All exhibits may be viewed closely, and the staff have considerable knowledge of the particular subjects which are their speciality. Whenever possible stewards give guided tours. Photographic displays explain the construction of the Mosquito – a wooden airplane built in the furniture factories by men and women who only months earlier had been manufacturing chairs and tables. The evolution of the Mosquito is shown by the BE2 and Hornet Moth up to the modern airliner – the Trident. On display are the prototype Mosquito, 15 De Haviland planes, many Rolls Royce engines and a completed nose section of a Horsa glider. A memorabilia exhibition shows Second World War life with gas masks, ration books and photographs of civilians and service personnel.

All displays may be closely examined and restoration work is often in progress.

Educational provision
Worksheets are in preparation and a museum brochure is available – price £1.

Shop
Shop open during museum hours sells books, aircraft kits, pens, hats and confectionary.

Disabled
Two wheelchairs available and all displays accessible except for the Trident and shop. A future new complex will accommodate wheelchairs.

MOUNT PLEASANT SORTING OFFICE

Farringdon Road, London EC1A 1BB
Tel: 01-278 5149

Underground: Farringdon
British Rail: Euston and Kings Cross

Open
Mon to Thurs for tours commencing at 10.30 a.m., 2.30 p.m. and 7.30 p.m.

Closed Fri, Sat and Sun, and from mid-Nov 1985 to mid-Jan 1986.

Admission charges
Free.

Mount Pleasant Sorting Office is one of the country's largest, with modern sorting and coding machines. The tour traces a letter's journey from the moment the stamp is licked to its final delivery. Coding machines change the postcode into dots which are read by the sorting machines. From the sorting office the letters drop down a chute, with specially slowed down bends, into the Post Office's own unique underground railway system built in the 1930s. Visitors can see how this automatic railway operates from London's railway stations and sorting offices, travelling at 35 mph between stops in order to avoid lost time in London's congested traffic above. This narrow-guage railway carries the tagged mail in small coaches and its control-board, which shows where each train is at that moment, is one of the highlights of the tour.

Educational provision
For teachers, information about the Post Office in general is available from the Regional Publicity Officer, 148-166 Old Street, London EC1V 9HQ.

MOTOR MUSEUM

(See British Motor Industry Heritage Trust.)

MUDCHUTE PARK AND FARM

Pier Street, Isle of Dogs, London E14
Tel: 01-515 5901

Underground: Mile End

Open

9.30 a.m. – 5 p.m. or until dark Daily.
Never closed.

Admission charges

Free.

Mudchute Park and Farm has 32 acres of open space
incorporating a pony club and farm. The farm animals
include cows, sheep (including Jacob sheep), pigs (including a
Tamworth sow), goats and fowl. A wide variety of birds can be
seen including the skylark. There are views across the river to
Greenwich, Tower Bridge, St Paul's and the GPO tower.
Visitors can give general help around the farm, feed the
animals and take part in tree planting from November to
March.

Educational provision

Visits round the farm are escorted and a classroom and
teachers' pack are available.

Shop

Shop open 10 a.m. – 4 p.m. (winter) and 10 a.m. – 6 p.m.
(summer) sells light refreshments, farm produce and books
including *Farm in a City* and *Wildlife on the Mudchute*.

MUSEUM OF ARTILLERY IN THE ROTUNDA

Repository Road, Woolwich, London SE18
Tel: 01-856 5533 extension 385

British Rail: Woolwich Dockyard

Open

Apr–Oct   12 noon – 5 p.m. Mon to Fri; 1 – 5 p.m. Sat and Sun.

Nov–Mar   12 noon – 4 p.m. Mon to Fri; 1 – 4 p.m. Sat and Sun.

Closed 24, 25, 26, 31 Dec, 1 Jan, Good Friday.

Admission charges
Free.

The **Museum of Artillery in the Rotunda** displays common weapons and equipment from medieval times to the present day. It has collections of arms, weapons, ammunition and radar systems. The Nash Rotunda tent, which houses the Museum, was originally erected for the Peace of Europe Celebrations in 1816.

Educational provision
There is a free audio-visual exhibit, a listening post, and four other audio-visual exhibits for which a small charge is made.
   Worksheets are available.

Refreshments
Vending machines sell hot and cold drinks. There is an open picnic area.

Shop
Open during museum hours selling postcards, prints, books and models.

MUSEUM OF GARDEN HISTORY

(See Tradescant Museum of Garden History.)

MUSEUM OF INSTRUMENTS

(See Royal Academy of Music.)

MUSEUM OF LONDON

London Wall, London EC2Y 5HN
Tel: 01-600 3699

Underground: Barbican, St Paul's and Moorgate

Open
10 a.m. – 6 p.m. Tues to Sat; 2.30 – 6 p.m. Sun.
Closed Mon.

Admission charges
Free. Booking essential for all parties.

The **Museum of London** tells the story of London and
Londoners from the earliest times until the present day. The
permanent galleries record the Prehistoric, Roman, Medieval,
Tudor, Stuart, Georgian, Victorian and 20th century
developments of London. The displays illustrate the growth of
the city and the ever-changing pattern of London life. Using an
open-plan design each gallery provides a wide range of
educational resources: artefacts, costume, documents,
contemporary illustrations, reconstructions, models and
music all combine to create the historic setting of the lives and
work of Londoners. There are also changing exhibitions
showing facets of London not covered in the main exhibition.

Educational provision
Three months prior booking is essential. The Education
Department contains a lecture theatre, classrooms,
cloakrooms, lunch-room and teachers' library. The
department provides gallery lists, worksheets (for which a
small charge is made) and book lists. General Teaching
Sessions are provided for any visiting group on the gallery
themes. These sessions include slides and the handling of
authentic material.

Refreshments
Cafeteria open during museum hours.

Shop

Shop open during museum hours sells postcards, books and souvenirs relating to London's history.

Disabled

Special help and advice is given to the disabled; all floors are accessible by lift.

MUSEUM OF MANKIND

6 Burlington Gardens, London W1X 2EX
Tel: 01-437 2224

Underground: Piccadilly Circus and Green Park

Open

10 a.m. – 5 p.m. Mon to Sat; 2.30 – 6 p.m. Sun.
Closed Christmas Day, Boxing Day, Good Friday, Easter Monday.

Admission charges

Free.

The **Museum of Mankind** focuses on non-Western cultures and lifestyles. From its wide collection it produces exhibitions which are constantly changing, showing a small part (as space is restricted) of the whole collection under a thematic title.

Exhibitions

For details of future events, phone the Museum.

Educational provision

Worksheets for the 11-15 age group are available, also teachers' notes for major exhibitions. Films and videos can be booked, and handling objects are available in connection with some exhibitions. There is a school's room for study periods and lunchtimes (packed lunches only).

Shop

Shop open 10.30 a.m. – 12.30 p.m. and 1.30 – 4.30 p.m. sells books, records, slides, postcards, models, clothing – all related to the museum.

Disabled

Lifts and ramps are provided and handling sessions and talks for the disabled can be arranged.

MUSEUM OF THE ORDER OF ST JOHN

**St John's Gate, St John's Lane, Clerkenwell,
London EC1 4DA
Tel: 01-253 6644**

Underground: Farringdon

Open

10 a.m. – 6 p.m. Tues and Fri; 10 a.m. – 4 p.m. Sat; guided tours at 11 a.m. and 2.30 p.m.
Closed Mon, Wed and Thurs.

Admission charges

Free.

The **Museum of the Order of St John** is a series of rooms in a 16th century gatehouse. One room is devoted to the history of St John's Ambulance, founded in 1877, featuring old uniforms and equipment, memorabilia and photographs showing the role of the Ambulance service in both World Wars. Another room is about the Order of St John, and contains texts and illustrations, following its history from the times of the Crusades. On display are paintings, silver, porcelain, glass and pharmacy jars. The coin and medal room has collections of coins from the Crusades, medals of the Knights of St John, seals, insignia, portraits and silver. In the library, a room in the 16th century St John's Gate, visitors can see historic leather-bound volumes.

The Grand Priory Church dates from about 1140 and contains historical items from the locality dating from the 16th century onwards. The Norman crypt is one London's rare Romanesque survivals.

Educational provision
Guided tours can be arranged for school parties.

Shop
Shop open 10 a.m. – 6 p.m. (4 p.m. on Sat) sells books, cards and souvenirs.

NATIONAL ARMY MUSEUM

Royal Hospital Road, London SW3 4HT
Tel: 01-730 0717

Underground: Sloane Square

Open
10 a.m. – 5.30 p.m. Mon to Sat; 2 – 5.30 p.m. Sun.
Closed Christmas Day, Boxing Day, New Year's Day and May Day.

Admission charges
Free.

The **National Army Museum** is concerned with the history of the British Army from 1485 to 1982 and former colonial forces, especially those serving in India. There are five galleries devoted to Art, Uniform, Arms, the Army 1485 to 1914 and the Army 1914 to 1982.

There are gallery trails and quiz sheets available during school holidays. Special summer holiday events include plastic model-making, films, talks, etc.

Educational provision
For educational groups the museum provides free handling material for all ages and abilities with illustrated talks. There are special academic lectures for 6th formers and advice for teachers and students.

Shop
Shop open during museum hours sells postcards, books, posters, badges and puzzles.

Disabled
For the disabled there are special toilets, lifts to every gallery and ramps to the weapons gallery.

NATIONAL GALLERY

Trafalgar Square, London WC2N 5DN
Tel: 01-839 3321 and 01-839 3526 (recorded information)

Underground: Charing Cross, Leicester Square and Piccadilly Circus

Open
10 a.m. – 6 p.m. Mon to Sat; 2 – 6 p.m. Sun.
Closed Christmas Eve, Christmas Day, New Year's Day, Good Friday and May Day.

Admission charges
Free.

The **National Gallery** houses one of the world's greatest collections of pictures with over 2,000 paintings by Western European artists from about 1250 to 1900. The works are arranged in schools and include works by Rembrandt, Rubens, Uccello, Titian, Botticelli, Velasquez, van Eyck,

Holbein, Hogarth, Canaletto, Goya, Raphael, Michelangelo, Gainsborough, Monet, Picasso, Cézanne, Renoir and Rousseau. Among the many very famous works are *The Hay Wain* by Constable, *The Fighting Temeraire* by Turner, Leonardo da Vinci's cartoon *Virgin and Child*, and *Sunflowers* by Van Gogh.

There are lectures, guided tours and films for the general public and also for children, with worksheets and quizzes.

Special events
For details of future events, phone the Gallery.

Educational provision
Worksheets are available and there is a Sandwich Room which must be booked well in advance. The Gallery's Schools' Officers can give advice on how the study of the pictures can be incorporated into work being done at school. Talks on any aspect of the collection may be booked, and each is tailored to the requirements of the particular group.

Refreshments
Restaurant open 10 a.m. – 5 p.m. Mon to Sat; 2 – 5 p.m. Sun.

Shop
Shop open 10 a.m. – 5.40 p.m. Mon to Sat; 2 – 5.40 p.m. Sun sells catalogues and guides to the Collection, black and white photos of every painting, a selection of prints and slides, and posters and art books.

Disabled
A limited number of wheelchairs are available and lifts are at the Orange Street entrance. There is access to the whole of the collection; large parties are asked to phone in advance.

NATIONAL MARITIME MUSEUM

Greenwich, London SE10 9NF
Tel: 01-858 4422 extension 277

British Rail: Maze Hill

Open

Winter   10a.m. – 5 p.m. Mon to Fri; 10 a.m. – 5.30 p.m. Sat;
2 – 5 p.m. Sun.
Summer   10a.m. – 6 p.m. Mon to Sat; 2 – 5.30 p.m. Sun.
Closed Christmas Eve, Christmas Day, Boxing Day,
New Year's Day, Good Friday and May Day. Plus occasional
extra days around Christmas.

Admission charges

Per site: Main Buildings or Old Royal Observatory.
Children   2-site 75p, 1-site 50p.
Adults   2-site £1.50 1-site £1.
OAP, UB40 and *40p local ticket*   half price.
School Parties
50p per child with one free adult per 10 children.

The **National Maritime Museum** brings to life the crucial role
the sea has played in British History since earliest times. The
collections are housed in buildings which are themselves quite
outstanding. The central building, the Queen's House was
built by Inigo Jones, and the Old Royal Observatory by Sir
Christopher Wren. The Museum shows how water transport
developed from prehistoric log boats through the first
galleons, great men-o-war and Victorian iron steamers to
modern warships and merchantmen. There are many actual
boats and hundreds of detailed models. The collection of
compasses, telescopes, sextants, maps and charts includes the
28-inch refractor telescope housed in the 'onion Dome' near
the Greenwich Meridian. The brass line passing through the
Meridian Room is longitude zero – the centre of the world.
Personal items in the museum include the bullet-holed coat
that Nelson died in and the household effects of Captain Cook.

The museum is also an important art gallery with several thousand paintings with many notable works commemorating famous seafarers and naval battles.

Educational provision

School parties are asked to book in advance to make sure that children and teachers gain most from their visit. Films and illustrated talks can be given by prior arrangement, and worksheets and teachers' notes are available. The Museum's junior centre contains a studio for practical work and a mess deck for eating packed lunches. Planetarium programmes can be selected from a list of subjects and are free (public programmes are given on certain dates in the summer and there is a small admission charge).

Refreshments

Dolphin Coffee Shop open during museum hours serves tea, coffee, snacks and lunches.

Shop

Two museum bookshops open during museum hours sell books, prints, slides, postcards, replica instruments, jewellery, model kits, ship's badges and souvenirs.

Disabled

Toilets for disabled and limited access to galleries by ramps.

NATIONAL MUSEUM OF LABOUR HISTORY

Limehouse Town Hall, Commercial Road, London E14 7HA

Tel: 01-515 3229

British Rail: Stepney East

Open

9.30 a.m. – 5 p.m. Tues to Sat; 2.30 – 5.30 p.m. Sun.
Closed Mon, and one week at Christmas.

Admission charges

Free.

The **National Museum of Labour History** is unique in Britain in offering a true 'People's History' in archival and visual form from the industrial revolution to the present day. Visitors can come to study, learn or simply see and enjoy the presentation of the collection of memorabilia of the British Trade Union and Labour Movements. The museum has a specialised library of photographs dating from the 1840s, and is among the most comprehensive photographic libraries of social and labour history in the country. The museum has some 60 Trade Union banners, which are being restored, and at any one time about 15 are on display.

Educational provision

The museum runs a varied educational programme sponsored by the ILEA and other educational institutions. It offers lectures from CSE to 'A' level, and also runs evening classses and lectures to schools. Pamphlets for school students are on sale.

Shop

Bookstall open during museum hours sells posters, pamphlets, books, postcards and cartoons.

NATIONAL PORTRAIT GALLERY

St Martin's Place, London WC2H 0HE
Tel: 01-930 1552

Underground: Leicester Square and Charing Cross
British Rail: Charing Cross

Open

10 a.m. – 5 p.m. Mon to Fri; 10 a.m. – 6 p.m. Sat; 2 – 6 p.m. Sun. Closed Good Friday, May Day, 24, 25 and 26 Dec, New Year's Day.

Admission charges

Free except for certain special exhibitions..

The **National Portrait Gallery** was founded in 1856 with the aim of collecting the likenesses of famous British men and women from the Tudor times to the present day. The collection is arranged chronologically, beginning on the top floor with the Middle Ages and the Tudors, ending with the 20th century galleries on the ground floor, opened earlier this year. Each room has been given a particular historical theme. Furnishings, maps, engravings, weapons and other materials have been included to set portraits in a historical context, and to provide a narrative framework. The Gallery offers a unique panorama of British history as unfolded through the personalities of its great men and women, kings and queens, scholars and statesmen, soldiers and poets, scientists and explorers. The primary collection numbers some thousand portraits comprising oil paintings, water-colours, drawings, miniatures, sculpture, caricatures, silhouettes, photographs and videos.

Regular features are exhibitions on a wide variety of historical, biographical and artistic subjects including the annual competition for young artists – the John Player Portrait Award; other events include holiday activities held for children, public lectures, room talks and exhibition talks for adults and older children.

Special events
For details of future events, phone the Gallery.

Educational provision
Worksheets are freely available to the public on request; the Education Department provides for many age groups, including sixth formers and college students, primary and secondary age groups as well as adult education. Its many activities include general introductions to the Gallery, approaches to temporary exhibitions and practical art lessons.

Teachers' courses are held to introduce teaching staff to the consolidated teaching programmes.

Shop
Shop open during museum hours sells catalogues, postcards, Gallery publications, books, greetings cards, calendars, notepads, badges, bookmarks, black and white photographs and slides of exhibits and other souvenirs.

Disabled
There are toilets for the disabled and entry to the Gallery via the entrance in Orange Street (advance notice necessary). There is a short flight of stairs from the main entrance to the lift and help with these is available from Warding Staff.

NATIONAL POSTAL MUSEUM

King Edward Building, King Edward Street, London EC1A 1LP
Tel: 01-432 3851

Underground: St Paul's

Open
10 a.m. – 4.30 p.m. Mon to Thurs; 10 a.m. – 4 p.m. Fri. Closed Sat and Sun, Bank holidays, Public holidays and 7-13 Oct for repairs.

Admission charges
Free.

The **National Postal Museum** houses the Reginald Phillips collection of Victoriana, stamps and essays. There are 1 penny blacks, 2 penny blues, stamp trials, stamps on envelopes and embossed stamps on covers. The Universal Postal Union collection of stamps of the world is also on display, and throughout the year there are special exhibitions dealing with a Post Office theme.

Questionnaires on the exhibitions on current display are

available and the answers are hidden in the display – participants will have to locate them by carefully looking at the display articles.

Special events
For details of future events, phone the Museum.

Educational provision
A lecture room includes a cinema and films are shown on postal subjects to school parties and groups. Guided tours are also available but these must be prebooked.

Shop
Sales counter selling museum-produced postcards which are issued in conjunction with the exhibitions, postcard albums, First Day Covers and various books on philately.

NATIONAL THEATRE

South Bank, London SE1 9PX
Tel: 01-928 2033

Underground: Waterloo
British Rail: Waterloo

Open
Mon to Sat Tours start 10.15 a.m., 12.30 a.m. (not Wed or Sat), 12.45 p.m., 5.30 p.m. (not Wed or Sat) and 6 p.m.
Closed Sun.

Admission charges
Tour charges   £2 per person.
Students   £1.50.
Party rates
£1.50 per person if number over 15.
£1.10 per person for 30 (max size) if member of groups association.

The **National Theatre** puts on three plays daily in three auditoria, and there are foyer events most days. The tour of the theatre, which takes 1 to 1 1/2 hours, starts from the Littleton information desk and covers the three auditoria, backstage, and the workshop area. A broadsheet is available with facts and figures and details of theatre and productions.

The Maugham Collection of Theatrical Paintings is displayed in the foyer and corridors from 10 a.m. – 11 p.m., no charge. Paintings include *Drury Lane Theatre 1824-5* by Samuel de Wild, and *Alexander Pope as Dumont in the Tragedy of Jane Shaw* by Nicholas Rowe.

Refreshments
Box Office Buffet open from 10 a.m. – 11 p.m., Littleton Buffet 12 noon – 8 p.m., Olivier Buffet subject to performances in Olivier Theatre.

Shop
Shop open from 10 a.m. – 11 p.m. sells books, catalogues, postcards, greetings cards and play scripts.

Disabled
Special toilets. The tour is accessible to the disabled but it is better to come as a pre-booked group than individually.

NATURAL HISTORY MUSEUM

Cromwell Road, South Kensington, London SW7 5BD
Tel: 01-589 6323

Underground: South Kensington

Open

10 a.m. – 6 p.m. Mon to Sat; 2.30 – 6 p.m. Sun.
Closed Christmas Day, Boxing Day and some Bank holidays, including May Day.

Admission charges

Free.

The **Natural History Museum** has an extensive range of permanent exhibitions. The more recent ones include Human Biology, Dinosaurs and their Living Relatives, Introducing Ecology, Origin of the Species, Man's Place in Evolution, and Classification and British Natural History. Also featured in exhibitions are Birds, Insects, Marine Invertebrates, Fossils, Mammals, Minerals and Meteorites.

There are activity and information sheets to find out more about natural history when viewing the exhibitions. During the Easter vacation and August children can go to the family centre and handle specimens, undertake hands-on activities and learn more about natural history. There is a regular programme of public lectures and films at 3 p.m. on Tuesdays, Thursdays and Saturdays.

Educational provision

Activity sheets and written material for school groups are available and must be ordered at least 2 weeks before the visit. Tours of the galleries for 7 to 11 year olds are given by trained volunteers. There are special Christmas lectures to sixth formers and a regular programme of teachers' courses on how to use the museum, including courses for student teachers.

Refreshments

One cafeteria and one restaurant open from 10 a.m. – 5.10 p.m. Children's parties can be catered for if booked in advance.

Shop

A shop, bookshop and souvenir counter, open from 10 a.m. – 5.40 p.m. selling postcards, books ,souvenirs, gifts for all ages, and some audio-visual teaching aids.

Disabled
Limited facilities include toilets, special lifts and help from staff.

NORTH WOOLWICH RAILWAY MUSEUM

Old Station, Pier Road, North Woolwich, London E16 2JJ
Tel: 01-534 0276

British Rail: North Woolwich

Open
10 a.m. – 5 p.m. Mon to Sat; 2 – 5 p.m. Sun.
Closed Christmas Eve and Christmas Day.

Admission charges
Free.

The **North Woolwich Railway Museum** is the museum of the Great Eastern Railway. It includes artefacts, photographs and documents of that railway company. There is a complete ticket office and currently one full-size locomotive is on show. By the Spring of 1985 live steam should be on show.

Educational provision
There is a lecture room and conducted tours, talks and lectures can be provided by arrangement.

Shop
Shop open from 10 a.m. – 4.45 p.m. selling books, kits, posters, pens, pencils and badges.

Disabled
There is easy access to all facilities which are on the ground floor.

OLD BAILEY

London EC4 7EH
Tel: 01-248 3277

Underground: St Paul's

Open
10.15 a.m. – 4 p.m. Mon to Fri.
Closed Sat, Sun and Bank holidays.

Admission charges
Free.

The Public Galleries of the Central Criminal Court are open
during trials. Where famous cases are being tried there is
obviously limited space, but at other times the public is free to
enter the galleries and watch criminal trials in progress.

Disabled
Limited facilities for the disabled exist.

OLD BATTERSEA HOUSE

Vicarage Crescent, London SW13
Tel: None.

British Rail: Clapham Junction

Open
Wed p.m. by appointment only.

Admission charges
Children 50p.
Adults 50p.

Old Battersea House is the finest example of 17th century
domestic architecture existing in the area. It is presumed to
have been built in 1699, the date on the sundail fixed to the

South face, on Tudor foundations. In style it is typical of the many brick houses built in London in the second half of the 17th century. The Forbes foundation has restored the house and opened a part of the ground floor where visitors also have the opportunity to see the De Morgan Collection of pottery, paintings and porcelain. Evelyn De Morgan (1855-1919), influenced first by the Italian primitives and later by the pre-Raphaelites, was regarded as a spiritual and deeply sincere artist in her lifetime. She is represented by about 80 paintings and a large portfolio of drawings. Her husband, William De Morgan decorated pottery and porcelain with a richness of pattern and colour that has never been equalled in the country. His early designs show strongly the influence of William Morris; later he tried to imitate the rich blue and turquoise glazes of Turkey, Persia and Syria. He also rediscovered the techniques of lustre that had been first used in Persia in the 13th century and had died out in Italy three centuries later. By the mid-1870s no fashionable house was complete without its William Morris wallpapers or De Morgan tiles.

OLD CURIOSITY SHOP

13-14 Portsmouth Street, London WC2A 2ES
Tel: 01-405 9891

Underground: Holborn

Open
9.30 a.m. – 5.30 p.m. Daily.
Closed Christmas Day.

Admission charges
Free.

The **Old Curiosity Shop** is the oldest shop in London – it was built in 1567. The premises were originally two tiny shops with a room over each, and there are separate staircases. The shop was immortalised by Dickens and it is still used for the same purpose as it was in the book – all kinds of old and curious articles can be bought. The dividing partition between the shop and the sitting room has had to be removed, but otherwise the building remains the same as it was in Dickens' time. One fireplace upstairs is original and was uncovered only a few years ago. A number of Dickens' mementoes can be seen, including a photograph album which once belonged to Nancy Cornelius, an old servant and friend of the Dickens' family.

Educational provision
Pamphlets are available on request.

Shop
Shop sells antiques and Dickens souvenirs.

OLD PALACE, CROYDON

Old Palace Road, Croydon, Surrey
Tel: 01-680 5877

British Rail: East Croydon and West Croydon

Open
Apr 9-13, May 28 – June 1, July 15-20 and July 22-27   for conducted tours only at 2.30 p.m. (doors open 2 p.m.). Two weeks notice for party visits.

Admission charges
(which includes home-made tea served in the Undercroft).
Children   £1 (*Note:* the tour would only be of interest to children over 12).
Adults   £1.50.

The **Old Palace, Croydon**, former residence of the Archbishops of Canterbury dates back over one thousand years. In Saxon times it was called a manor and its Lord was the Archibishop of Canterbury. The Archbishops must have used the Palace as a country residence and as the ·

180

headquarters when engaged on diocesan business. Two saints at some time lived here – Anselm and Thomas à Becket. There have been many royal visitors – Edward I, Henry VII (courting Katherine of Aragon), Mary Tudor and Queen Elizabeth I, whose bedroom can be seen. In the medieval Guard Room King James I of Scotland was kept prisoner for fourteen years. The chapel was built in Tudor times and the Undercroft, where tea is taken, is Norman.

Educational provision
On sale is a reprint of two articles from *Country Life*, which give a complete history of the Old Palace.

Shop
Shop open at the end of each tour sells souvenirs.

OLD ROYAL OBSERVATORY

(See National Maritime Museum.)

OLD ST THOMAS OPERATING THEATRE AND HERB GARRET

Guy's Hospital, Counting House, St Thomas Street, London SE1 9RT
Tel: 01-407 7600 extensions 2739 and 3140

Underground: London Bridge
British Rail: London Bridge

Open
12.30 – 4 p.m. Mon, Wed and Fri. Other times by appointment.
Closed two weeks in August and December.

Admission charges
Children   35p.
Adults   70p.

OAP and Student   35p.
School Parties
35p per person in normal opening hours and 15p per person
out-of-hours by arrangement with the Curator.

The **Old St Thomas Operating Theatre** is unique in being the
only one to survive from the pre-antiseptic days. It was built in
1821, used for 40 years and then bricked up, being rediscovered
in 1956 and opened as a museum piece in 1962, exactly 100
years after it had ceased to be used for surgery. Other London
hospitals provided the authentic operating room furniture. In
the Herb Garret are exhibits illustrative of some aspects of
surgery, pharmacy and nursing. The museum gives a
fascinating insight into the history of medicine.

Educational provision
A half-hour lecture is given to all pre-booked organised
groups.

Shop
Postcards and other literature are available from the Curator.

OLD SPEECH ROOM GALLERY

**Harrow School, 15 London Road, Harrow-On-The-Hill,
Middlesex HA1 3JJ
Tel: 01-422 2303**

Underground: Harrow-On-The-Hill

Open
By appointment on almost any day in term-time or by special
arrangement in the holidays.
Tours normally begin between 10 and 11 a.m. or 2 and 4 p.m.

Admission charges
Short Tour (1 hour)
Children   80p.
Adults   £1.30.
OAP   80p.

Standard Tour (1½ hours)
Children £1.
Adults £1.60.
OAP £1.
Full Tour (2 hours)
Children £1.25.
Adults £2.
OAP £1.25
(Child rates are for children accompanying their parents).
School Parties
as child rate with one free teacher per 15 children.

The **Old Speech Room Gallery** was built in 1820 as an
assembly room to enable visitors to hear the annual speech
making by the boys and it was converted in 1976 into a
Museum and Art Gallery, and now contains many of the
School's treasures on public display. The magnificent
collection of Greek and Etruscan pots was donated by an Old
Boy, and the collection of water-colours by a number of
distinguished artists. The exhibits vary from time to time and
each term special exhibitions are mounted. All the tours
include a visit to the Fourth Form Room which is a
well-preserved Jacobean schoolroom with its panelled walls
covered with the names of former pupils including Byron,
Sheridan, Trollope, Robert Peel and Winston Churchill.
Visitors see other old and modern school buildings, including
the modern dining hall which won an award for architecture
in 1980.

Shop
Shop open after tours sells guide books, postcards, sweatshirts,
mugs and souvenirs.

ORLEANS HOUSE GALLERY

Riverside, Twickenham, Middlesex TW11 3DJ
Tel: 01-892 0221

British Rail: Twickenham or St Margarets

Open

Apr – Sept 1 – 5.30 p.m. Tues to Sat; 2 – 5.30 p.m. Sun,
Spring and August bank holidays.
Oct – Mar 1 – 4.30 p.m. Tues to Sat; 2 – 4.30 p.m. Sun.
Closed Mon except Spring and August Bank holidays.

Admission charges

Free.

Orleans House Gallery has a changing programme on a wide
range of subjects.

Special events

For details of future events, phone the Gallery.

Educational provision

Worksheets are prepared for special exhibitions, particularly
those on local themes.

Shop

Publications are available for purchase during normal
opening hours – postcards, greeting cards, reproduction
prints, exhibition catalogues, miscellaneous library
publications and leaflets.

Disabled

Ramp access to the ground floor of the building only. Special
toilets are available.

ORPINGTON MUSEUM

(See Bromley Museum.)

OSTERLEY PARK HOUSE (National Trust)

Osterley Park, Osterley, Middlesex
Tel: 01-560 3918

Underground: Osterley

Open
Oct – Mar   12 noon – 4 p.m. Tues to Sun.
Apr – Sept   2 – 6 p.m. Tues to Sun.
Closed Mon.

Admission charges
Children   75p.
Adults   £1.50.
OAP, UB40 and pre-booked groups   75p.
School Parties
Free.

Osterley Park House is the 18th century home of the Child banking family, with original Robert Adam decoration, and fine furniture and tapestries. It has an Elizabethan stable block and a fine 18th century landscaped park with garden buildings.

Refreshments
Cafeteria open from April to September.

Disabled
There are toilets for the disabled and wheelchairs are available in the house.

PACKET, PORTABELLA

Portabella Docks, Ladbroke Grove, London W10
Tel: 01-937 7994

Underground: Ladbroke Grove

Open
Opening and closing times are flexible – the Packet is booked for the trip.

Admission charges
£89 per trip under 3 hours. Over 3 hours, negotiable.

The **Packet** cruises up the Grand Union Canal between Portabella Docks and Camden Lock in one direction and as far out as Park Royal in the other. On the way to Camden the boat passes Browning's Island, Little Venice and Regents Park Zoo. Moving down towards Park Royal out of London it is possible to stop off on the way for a pre-arranged barbecue or picnic. The Packet is a traditionally painted narrow boat which can hold up to 60 people for drinks and finger buffet. Trips are individually tailored and can include on-board music.

Educational provision
Sightseeing commentary for school parties.

PARADISE PARK AND WOODLAND ZOO

White Stubbs Lane, Broxbourne, Herts.
Tel: (Hoddesdon) 0992 468001

British Rail: Broxbourne

Open
10 a.m. – 6 p.m. Daily.
Never closed.

Admission charges
Children   50p (3 or under free).
Adults   £1.
School Parties   Discounts by arrangement.

Paradise Park and Woodland Zoo is reopening in the summer of 1985. It has monkeys, goats, guanacos, donkeys, ponies, wolves, a lion and a Vietnamese Pot-bellied pig, and more animals will be purchased as soon as rebuilding is completed. There is a picnic area, train ride, and a woodland walk.

A restaurant and shops (selling gifts, sweets and ice-creams) are also being completed.

Disabled
Toilets are being built and paths levelled.

PARK LODGE FARM CENTRE

Park Lodge Farm, Harvil Road, Harefield, Middlesex
Tel: (Harefield) 089 582 4425

British Rail: Denham

Open
10 a.m. – 4 p.m. Mon to Fri for school parties only.
Closed on Sat and Sun.

Admission charges
School Parties
£17.50 per 50.

Park Lodge Farm Centre has 500 acres with 200 milking cows, 180 young stock, 180 ewes and 300 lambs. This is a chance to see a real farm at work which is also participating in countryside conservation projects. Milking can be seen daily, lambing in March and April and calvings from August to December. There is a nature trail and a collection of agricultural bygones. Learning by sight, smell and touch is very much encouraged.

Educational provision

Teachers must come on a preliminary visit to the Centre – this is compulsory. There are lecture rooms and information sheets are provided for teachers.

PASSMORE EDWARDS MUSEUM

Romford Road, Stratford, London E15 4LZ
Tel: 01-519 4296 and 01-534 4545 extension 5670

Underground: Stratford

Open
10 a.m. – 6 p.m. Mon to Sat; 2 – 5p.m. Sun.
Closed Bank holidays.

Admission charges
Free.

The **Passmore Edwards Museum** is concerned with the heritage of the geographical County of Essex in the fields of archaeology and local history, biology and geology.

The Bottom Gallery covers natural history with representative species from all divisions of the animal kingdom as found in Essex, from worms, slugs and jellyfish to birds and mammals. The exhibits are arranged in order of ascending development starting with primitive animals and progressing to the more developed ones.

The Museum's Upper Gallery is divided into two sections – archaeology and local history. The first covers the archaeology of the five boroughs east of the Lea and spans from paleolithic (earliest stone age) through bronze and iron ages, Roman, Saxon and Medieval with a post-Medieval section on early technology and timber building.

The Waltham Abbey Bible is one of the star exhibits and there is much recently discovered material including some finds from Mucking.

The local history section depicts daily life in the area –

education and childhood, vernacular architecture and pastimes. There is a fine collection of Bow porcelain made in the Bow factory on the edges of Stratford.

Educational provision
Teachers' guides, lectures and many other educational requirements supplied by the Extension Services Section of the museum.

Shop
Shop open during museum hours sells books, pens, pencils, souvenirs, colouring sheets and books.

PATRICK COOK'S MUSEUM

(See Bakelite Museum.)

PEOPLE'S FARM

**108-122 Shacklewell Lane, Dalston, London E8
Tel: 01-806 5743**

British Rail: Dalston Kingsland Road

Open
9.30 a.m. – 6 p.m. Daily.
Never closed.

Admission charges
Free.

The **People's Farm** has a wide variety of livestock – calves, goats, fowl, pigs, horses, sheep, geese, ducks and peacocks. Visitors can see a working farm with farmyard management and animal husbandry. The animals are fed three times a day, roughly 9.30 a.m., 12 noon and 4.30 p.m. (later in the

summer). There are usually young or newly-born animals at
all seasons.

Shop
Eggs are sold all day.

Disabled
There is wheelchair access to most parts of the farm by
concrete paths.

PERCIVAL DAVID FOUNDATION OF CHINESE ART

53 Gordon Square, London WC1H 0PD
Tel: 01-387 3909

Underground: Russell Square
British Rail: Euston

Open
2.30 – 5 p.m. Mon; 10.30 a.m. – 5 p.m. Tues to Fri;
10.30 a.m. – 1 p.m. Sat.
Closed Sun, Sat during August, Bank holidays and preceding
Sat.

Admission charges
Free. Children must be accompanied.

The **David Collection** contains about 1500 pieces of Chinese
ceramics of the Sung, Yuan, Ming and Ch'ing dynasties.
Numerous inscribed pieces give the collection a special
importance in the history of ceramic art. Many are inscribed,
some with poetry, and are historical documents in their own
right. The beautiful blue and white ware from Ching-te-Chen
includes the earliest dated pieces (dated 1351) but also a fine
range from the 15th century. Polychrome wares are well-
represented from the 15th century onwards. There are also fine
monochrome porcelains, mainly dateable to the 18th century.

190

Educational provision
An introduction to the collection for educational groups can be arranged with the curator.

Shop
Sales desk open during Gallery hours sells postcards, slides and books.

Disabled
There are lifts and toilet facilities for the disabled but attention is drawn to the steps up to the front entrance.

PETERSHAM FARM

Petersham Road, Richmond, Surrey TW10 7AA
Tel: 01-948 3657

Underground: Richmond

Open
For school visits or groups by special arrangement only.

Admission charges
70p per person (unless very large school groups).

Petersham Farm has sheep, calves, an unusual Vietnamese pot-bellied pig, horses, goats and hens. These are non-battery hens and visitors can see egg production from them. There are also turkeys on the farm from August to December.

Shop
Shop open 9 a.m. – 5 p.m. sells eggs, goats' milk, and pork and lamb for the freezer.

PETRIE MUSEUM OF EGYPTIAN ARCHAEOLOGY

University College, Gower Street, London WC1E 6JP
Tel: 01-387 7050 extension 617

Underground: Euston Square, Goodge Street and Warren Street
British Rail: Euston

Open
10 a.m. – 5 p.m. Mon to Fri.
Closed Sat and Sun and 6 weeks in summer, one week at Christmas and one week at Easter.

Admission charges
Free.

The **Petrie Museum of Egyptian Archaeology** features all aspects of daily life in Ancient Egypt – dress, games, toys and writings. Also on display are Egyptian mummies, a skeleton in a burial pot, jewellery and Graeco-Roman portraits. Textiles from Egypt include the world's earliest dress, dated around 2800 BC, with two more dresses from around 2400 BC. There is also a collection of bronze Egyptian cats. In the college cloisters are the Koptos lions – monumental stone lions from Upper Egypt.

Guided tours for parties of around 15 can be provided by arrangement.

Educational provision
A general museum guidebook is available for 50p.

Refreshments
College refectories are open 9.15 – 11 a.m., 12 noon – 2 p.m., 3 – 5 p.m. and 5.30 – 7.15 p.m.

Shop
Shop open during museum hours sells guidebooks, egyptological publications, posters, postcards and slides.

Disabled
There is limited access with handrails from the pottery room
into the main museum.

PHOTOGRAPHERS' GALLERY

5 and 8 Great Newport Street, London WC2
Tel: 01-240 5511

Underground: Leicester Square

Open
11 a.m. – 7 p.m. Tues to Sat.
Closed Sun and Mon.

Admission charges
Children 30p.
Adults 50p.
OAP and UB40 free.
School Parties
by arrangement.

The **Photographers' Gallery** holds exhibitions of photographs
in both galleries, with three shows at all times. A varied
programme means that there may be theme exhibitions or
one-person shows, each running for about one month except
in July and August, and December and January when they run
for two months.

Educational provision
Newsheets and wall texts are always available and if arranged
in advance, staff can give talks to visiting students. The
Gallery hope to have an Education Officer in early 1985.

Refreshments
Coffee bar open from 12 noon – 6 p.m.

Shop
Bookshop in number 8 and Print Room in number 5 open
11 a.m. – 7 p.m. sell books, postcards, posters, catalogues and
photographic prints.

Disabled
Ramp at number 5 (ask at desk) and double doors with slight
step at number 8.

PLUMSTEAD MUSEUM

232 Plumstead High Street, London SE18 1JT
Tel: 01-855 3240

British Rail: Plumstead

Open
2 – 8 p.m. Mon; 10 a.m. – 1 p.m. and 2 – 5 p.m. Tues and Thurs
to Sat.
Closed Wed and Sun.

Admission charges
Free.

Plumstead Museum consists of two rooms devoted to the
natural history of the locality, with some archaeological
material and later history displays. Primarily, material is from
the Greenwich Borough area. The display area will be
increased in 1985.

Brass rubbing may be done by appointment.

Educational provision
School visits are encouraged by appointment and it is hoped
that there will be a new education room by Summer 1985. A
school loan service to the Borough operates.

Disabled
The Museum is upstairs with no facilities for the disabled.

POLKA CHILDREN'S THEATRE

240 The Broadway, Wimbledon, London SW19 1SB
Tel: 01-543 3063 and 01-543 4888

Underground: Wimbledon or South Wimbledon

Open
10 a.m. – 4.30 p.m. Tues to Fri; 12 noon – 6 p.m. (sometimes until 7.30) Sat.
Closed Sun and Mon, September and Christmas Day.

Admission charges
Vary according to the production and courses. Exhibition is free.

The **Polka Children's Theatre** was designed and purpose-built for children, marking the culmination of the work of POLKA from its founding in 1967 by director, Richard Gill and designer, Elizabeth Waghorn. POLKA started as a touring company and gained a reputation for excellence at home and abroad. But the work does not only include the production of delightful children's theatre, there is a World of Puppets exhibition which is a colourful and fascinating display of puppets from prehistoric shadow puppets to modern 'space age' puppets.

Educational provision
Polka offers a full range of workshops and courses in drama, puppetry, mask-making, mime, music, art, toy-making and many other themes. There are special courses for handicapped children, and courses for teachers. Quiz sheets for the exhibition can be ordered in advance at no extra charge and follow-up notes are available for teachers for each production. Tours can be booked.

Refreshments
The Polka Pantry is open during theatre hours.

Shop
Toy shop open during theatre hours sells a wide variety of pocket-money toys, hand-crafted toys and gifts.

Disabled
Wide doors, lift to auditorium, toilets, special front row seats,
induction loop, and workshops for the disabled are all
available.

POLLOCK'S TOY MUSEUM
1 Scala Street, London W1P 1 LT
Tel: 01-636 3452

Underground: Goodge Street

Open
10 a.m. – 5 p.m. Mon to Sat.
Closed Sun and Bank holidays.

Admission charges
Children   20p.
Adults   50p.
OAP and Student   20p.

Pollock's Toy Museum was started in 1956 and has since
expanded into two little houses joined together in an
intriguing way with narrow winding staircases. Its oldest
exhibit is 4,000 years old, and it displays many toys from the
Third World and America. There are dolls, dolls houses, teddy
bears, tin toys, optical toys, board games and toy theatres, and
some early comics and early jigsaws (invented in Britain in the
18th century). There are some familiar puppets and modern
space toys.

Occasional toy theatre performances are given in the school
holidays, and these may also be requested for visiting school
groups.

Educational provision
A free guide is given to all visitors. Teachers are recommended
to visit the museum in advance, and a brochure 'Pollock's
World of Toys', providing a useful background to the main
features of the museum, can be sent (send PO for £1).

196

Shop

Shop open 10 a.m. – 5 p.m. sells toy theatres, books, cut-outs, postcards, colouring books and a wide variety of toys.

PRINCE HENRY'S ROOM

17 Fleet Street, London EC4
Tel: 01-353 7323

Underground: Temple

Open
1.45 – 5 p.m. Mon to Fri; 1.45 – 4.30 p.m. Sat.
Closed Sun, Christmas Day, Good Friday and Bank holidays.

Admission charges
10p per person.

Prince Henry's Room is one of the few houses in London which survive today from before the Great Fire of London in 1666. In 1900 it was discovered that there was a false front on the building and behind this was the original 17th century half-timbered front which now appears in its original form. Inside the building the main feature of interest is the large room on the first floor. Originally panelled in oak, it is now panelled partly in oak and partly in pine. The great treasure of the house is the ceiling – one of the best remaining Jacobean enriched plaster ceilings in London.

Prince Henry's Room contains an exhibition of Pepysiana, with contemporary items, prints and paintings depicting Samuel Pepys and London of the 17 century in which he lived.

Shop
Literature and postcards are on sale.

PUBLIC RECORD OFFICE MUSEUM

Chancery Lane, London WC2
Tel: 01-405 3488 extension 475

Underground: Chancery Lane, Holborn and Temple

Open
1–4 p.m. Mon to Fri.
Closed weekends and Public holidays.

Admission charges
Free.

The **Public Record Office Museum** has examples of all types of records of national interest. Here are copies of the Magna Carta, Shakespeare's will, Royal autographs and Guy Fawkes' confession. Also on view are documents from the First and Second World Wars.

Educational provision
School parties can make special arrangements to visit in the mornings.

Shop
Shop open 1–4 p.m. sells postcards, slides, seal replicas and document facsimiles.

PUMPING STATIONS

(See Thames Water Sewage Treatment Works and Pumping Stations.)

PUPPET CENTRE

Battersea Arts Centre, Lavendar Hill, London SW11 5TS
Tel: 01-228 5335

British Rail: Clapham Junction

Open
2 – 6 p.m. Mon to Fri.
Closed weekends and Bank holidays.

Admission charges
Free.

The **Puppet Centre** is an information organisation supplying details and news of what is going on in the puppet world in London and throughout the country. The reference library has a large collection of books on puppetry and related theatre arts. The Centre also has a small exhibition of different types of puppets, and children do have the opportunity to try out a range of puppets. However, advance booking for this must be made.

Educational provision
There is a workshop and equipment for school groups, and demonstrations and workshops can be arranged if advance notice is given. A small charge may have to be made to cover expenses.

  Students also have access to study material including reports and theses.

Refreshments
Cafeteria open 10 a.m. – 2.30 p.m. Mon and Tues,
10 a.m. – 8 p.m. Wed to Fri.

Shop
Bookshop open Wed to Sun selling books, postcards and magazines.

QUEBEC HOUSE (National Trust)

Westerham. Kent TN16 1TD
Tel: (Westerham) 0959 62206

British Rail: Sevenoaks or Oxted

Open

Apr – Oct   2 – 6 p.m. Mon to Wed, Fri and Sun.
Mar   2 – 6 p.m. (last admission 5.30 p.m.) Sun only.
Closed Thurs and Sat and Nov to Feb.

Admission charges

Children   55p.
Adults   £1.10.
Pre-booked Parties
Children   40p.
Adults   80p.

Quebec House is a gabled red brick 17th century house with Tudor origins. General Wolfe, one of England's greatest soldiers spent his early years here. The walled garden and four rooms are on view, the latter containing portraits, prints and memorabilia relating to Wolfe and his family. In the Tudor stable block behind the house is an exhibition about the Battle of Quebec and the part played by Wolfe and his adversary, the Marquis de Montcalm.

QUEEN MARY RESERVOIR

(See Thames Water Reservoirs.)

QUEEN'S COTTAGE

Kew Gardens, Kew, Surrey
Tel: 01-940 3321

Underground: Kew Gardens
British Rail: Kew Bridge

Open

Apr – Sept   11 a.m. – 5.30 p.m. Sat, Sun and Bank holidays.
Closed Mon to Fri and from Oct to Mar.

Admission charges

Children 15p.

Adults 30p.

OAP 15p.

School Parties

free if booked 14 days in advance.

The **Queen's Cottage**, named after Queen Charlotte, was built about 1772 as a summer house for the Royal Family. In the Green Room tea parties were held and in the print room there are Hogarth prints. In the kitchen are implements from the period and a complete Royal Dinner Service.

Refreshments

Cafeteria as for Kew Gardens.

Shop

Shop in Kew Palace.

QUEENS GALLERY

Buckingham Palace, Buckingham Palace Road, London SW1

Tel: 01-930 4832 extension 351

Underground: Victoria

British Rail: Victoria

Open

11 a.m. – 5 p.m. Tues to Sat and Bank holidays;

2 – 5 p.m. Sun.

Closed Mon except Bank holidays and Oct and Nov 1985.

Admission charges

Children 40p.

Adults £1.

OAP and Student 40p.

The **Queens Gallery** is exhibiting the Royal Faberge Collection from March to September 1985. Faberge devoted his skills to supplying works of art for a royal and aristocratic clientele and the flowers, birds, curios, animals, cigarette cases, picture frames and Easter eggs were conceived first and foremost as presents. Queen Alexandra's part of the collection contains a series of portraits of the animals at Sandringham – not just pets and racehorses, but also farmyard livestock ranging from a shire horse to turkeys and pigs. Queen Mary tended to prefer curios and table ornaments to animals and some of the most important pieces, such as the three Easter eggs which will be on display, were acquired by her. King George V's principal addition to the collection took the form of cigarette cases, which are among Faberge's most satisfying creations. This exhibition brings together some of the finest works of art which Faberge ever made.

The Gallery closes after the end of the exhibition in September and re-opens in December 1985 with an exhibition of Leonardo da Vinci drawings.

Shop
Bookstall open during gallery hours sells catalogues, current exhibition postcards, previous exhibition postcards and various publications.

Disabled
Wheelchair access is almost impossible as there are stairs.

RANGER'S HOUSE

Chesterfield Walk, Blackheath, London SE10 8QX
Tel: 01-348 1286 (office) 01-853 0035 (house)

British Rail: Greenwich or Blackheath

Open
Apr – Sept   10 a.m. – 7 p.m. Daily.
Feb, Mar and Oct   10 a.m. – 5 p.m. Daily.
Nov – Jan   10 a.m. – 4 p.m. Daily.
Closed Good Friday, Christmas Eve and Christmas Day.

Admission charges
Free.

Ranger's House is a handsome red brick villa, built on the 'Waste' on the edge of Greenwich Park in 1688. Its most illustrious occupant was Philip, 4th Earl of Chesterfield, the statesman and author of the famous 'Letters' to his natural son. In 1815 the house became the official residence of the Ranger of Greenwich Park, and a succession of royal and noble residents have occupied the house, including General Lord Wolseley, who led the expedition sent to relieve General Gordon at Khartoum. Ranger's House was converted by the GLC to art gallery use in 1974.

The Suffolk Collection formed part of the family collections of the Earls of Suffolk and Berkshire. The chief attraction of this collection is the magnificent series of full-length Jacobean portraits by William Larkin, the group of royal portraits by Lely and others, and the remaining paintings from the collection of Old Masters.

The house is being furnished in the appropriate style and the magnificent pair of giltwood tables, made for the Earls of Shaftesbury, was recently purchased. There is also a selection of musical instruments lent by the Horniman Museum including their Dolmetsch collection.

Educational provision
An education programme is run by Gene Adams, Educational Adviser to the ILEA. It includes school and holiday projects, guides for young visitors, worksheets and painting and modelling work in the basement workshop. Children can dress in replica historical costume based on one of the portraits, see historical dancing and listen to historical music. The House won the Sandford Award for Museum Education in 1979. Packed lunches can be eaten in the basement workshop.

Disabled
Lift to ground floor and toilets.

ROYAL ACADEMY OF ARTS

Burlington House, Piccadilly, London W1
Tel: 01-734 9052

Underground: Green Park and Piccadilly Circus

Open
10 a.m. – 6 p.m. Daily.
Closed a few days over Christmas.

Admission charges
Vary depending on the exhibition.

The **Royal Academy of Arts** permanent collection includes a
number of paintings by Royal Academicians of the 18th, 19th
and 20th centuries, including the *Leaping Horse* by John
Constable and *Dumbarton Castle* by Turner. *The Tondo* by
Michaelangelo can be viewed by appointment as can those
works not on display – only a part of the collection is on view
at any one time.

Special events
For details of future exhibitions, phone the Academy.

Educational provision
In conjunction with major loan exhibitions there are lunch-
time lectures and educational conferences for teachers, sixth
formers, university and art college students.

Refreshments
Cafeteria open 10 a.m. – 5 p.m.

Shop
Shop open during visiting hours sells books, postcards, artists'
materials, magazines and slides.

Disabled
Ramp from courtyard up to front door and lift can be used by arrangement. Special day for disabled to visit the Summer Exhibition on August 26.

ROYAL AIR FORCE MUSEUM

Grahame Park Way, Hendon, London NW9 5LL
(Same site as Bomber Command and Battle of Britain Museums)
Tel: 01-205 2266

Underground: Colindale

Open
10 a.m. – 6 p.m. Mon to Sat; 2 – 6 p.m. Sun.
Closed Christmas Eve, Christmas Day, Boxing Day, New Year's Day, Good Friday and May Day.

Admission charges
Free.

The **Royal Air Force Museum** display contains a unique and historic collection of over 40 aircraft in a brilliantly lit exhibition hall. Surrounding galleries depict over 100 years of military aviation history. Among the aircraft shown are such famous types as the Sopwith Camel, Spitfire, Beaufighter, Canberra, Meteor and Hunter. The Camm Collection commemorates the famous aircraft designer, the late Sir Sydney Camm. The Galleries' exhibits include aero-engines, propellers, armament, instruments, photographs, uniforms, decorations, trophies and paintings. Whenever possible contemporary environment has been recreated – an RFC workshop, a World War One armament lecture, WRAF huts – so that the collections are presented authentically and yet dramatically.

From Monday to Friday at 1.30 p.m. a selection of films is shown of general aviation interest as well as some of particular educational value.

Educational provision

Sample worksheets for children of both primary and secondary age, for duplication, may be obtained from the Education Officer. Short introductory slide talks can be given by prior arrangement with the Education Officer, on weekdays only between 10 a.m. – 12.30 p.m.

Refreshments

Self-service cafeteria open from 10 a.m. – 5 p.m. Mon to Sat and 2 – 5 p.m. Sun. Children's menu on application. Picnic building seats 50.

Shop

Opens with museum and closes one hour earlier, sells postcards, posters, aviation books, plastic kits, slides and souvenirs.

Disabled

All parts of the museum are accessible by wheelchair.

ROYAL ARTILLERY REGIMENTAL MUSEUM

Old Royal Military Academy, Academy Road, Woolwich, London SE18
Tel: 01-856 5533 extension 2523

British Rail: Woolwich Dockyard

Open

10 a.m. – 12.30 p.m. and 2 – 4 p.m. Mon to Fri.
Closed Public holidays.

Admission charges

Free.

The **Royal Artillery Regimental Museum** tells the story of the Royal Artillery from 1716 to the present day. It houses paintings, prints, photographs and has a collection of uniforms.

Educational provision

There are two free audio exhibits.

Shop

Open during museum hours sells postcards.

ROYAL COLLEGE OF MUSIC
MUSEUM OF INSTRUMENTS

Royal College of Music, Prince Consort Road, London SW7 2BS
Tel: 01-589 3643

Underground: South Kensington

Open

Wed during term time 11 a.m.–4 p.m. by previous arrangement with the Curator. Maximum party size is 15, minimum age 14 – all children must be accompanied by an adult.
Closed at all other times.

Admission charges

Children   40p.
Adults   60p.
OAP and Student   40p.

At the **Museum of Instruments** there are nearly 500 exhibits, mostly European keyboard, stringed and wind instruments from the 16th to 19th centuries. A small ethnological section includes instruments from China, Japan, India, the Middle East and Africa.

There are many important instruments including the clavicytherium *c.*1480 (the earliest surviving stringed keyboard instrument), the Trasuntino harpsichord made in Venice in 1531, Handel's spinet and Haydn's clavichord. Other instruments include flutes, trumpets, trombones, clarinets, and bagpipes, some of which were played and owned by the famous. The brass section is small but contains a number of rare items.

Depending on provision, visitors may also have the opportunity to see rehearsals and advanced music study.

Educational provision
A 16 page A5 guide on the contents of the museum, with 14 illustrations, is now available, price £1.

Disabled
Access for the disabled is difficult.

ROYAL FUSILIERS MUSEUM

HM Tower of London, London EC3N 4AB
Tel: 01-480 6082

Underground: Tower Hill

Open
Mar – Oct   9.30 a.m. – 5.45 p.m. (last ticket 5 p.m.) Mon to Sat; 2 – 5.45 p.m. (last ticket 5 p.m.) Sun.
Nov – Feb   9.30 a.m. – 4.30 p.m. (last ticket 4 p.m.) Mon to Sat.
Closed Sun from Nov to Feb, Christmas Eve, Christmas Day, Boxing Day, New Year's Day and Good Friday.

Admission charges
20p per person.

The **Royal Fusiliers Museum** shows the history of the regiment from 1865 until today. On display are nine Victoria Crosses, including the original approved by Queen Victoria. There are uniforms, equipment, weapons (rifles of various types and years), and mementoes from various campaigns, notebooks and printed training manuals. Also there are various silver objects, including a large silver bowl presented to the regiment by King William IV.

Refreshments

Self-service restaurant open 9.30 a.m. – 4.30 p.m. in winter, and 9.30 a.m. – 7 p.m. in summer, sells snacks and ice cream. Some kiosks are situated on the Wharf. Packed lunches may be eaten here.

Shop

Two shops open during visiting hours sell guidebooks, postcards, gifts and souvenirs.

ROYAL HOSPITAL MUSEUM

(See Chelsea Royal Hospital Museum.)

ROYAL MEWS

Buckingham Palace, London SW1W 0QH
Tel: 01-930 4832 extension 634

Underground: Victoria
British Rail: Victoria

Open

2 – 4 p.m. Wed and Thurs.
Closed Fri to Tues and any day there is a carriage procession.

Admission charges

Children   15p.
Adults   30p.
OAP and Student   15p.

The **Royal Mews** houses the Queen's carriage horses, carriages, and harness used on all state occasions. The magnificent Gold State Coach, built in 1716, is used by sovereigns when Opening Parliament and was used by the

Queen for her Coronation Procession. It is drawn by eight grey horses, is 24 feet long and weighs 4 tons. It is richly decorated with paintings by Cipriani, and its harness is of red morocco leather. Also in the Mews is the Glass State Coach, used for Royal Weddings.

Shop
Shop open during visiting hours sells postcards, books, slides, posters and jigsaws.

Disabled
Special toilets for the disabled are available.

ROYAL MILITARY SCHOOL OF MUSIC MUSEUM

Kneller Hall, Whitton, Twickenham, Middlesex TW2 7DU
Tel: 01-898 5533

British Rail: Whitton

Open
By appointment only.
Closed mid-Dec to early Jan; mid-Aug to mid-Sept; Easter; Sat, Sun and Wed p.m.

Admission charges
Free.

The **Royal Military School of Music Museum** houses woodwind and brass instruments as used in military bands from mid-18th to 20th century. In particular it has a collection of ophicleides – early brass instruments. During certain periods there may be an opportunity to listen to band rehearsals and to visit classrooms – depending on the school's programme.

Student guides escort all parties.

Shop
Records and Kneller Hall souvenirs can be purchased from
the instrument store by arrangement.

ROYAL NATIONAL INSTITUTE FOR THE BLIND RESOURCE CENTRE

224 Great Portland Street, London W1N 6AA
Tel: 01-388 1266

Underground: Great Portland Street

Open
9 a.m. – 5.15 p.m. Mon to Thurs; 9 a.m. – 5 p.m. Fri;
9 a.m. – 12.30 p.m. Sat.
Closed Sun, Bank holidays (and their previous Sats).

Admission charges
Free.

The **RNIB Resource Centre** has aids to help blind people –
both those specially made for the RNIB, or adapted for the
blind and partially-sighted, and also some commercial aids.
Electronic equipment includes closed-circuit TV (which
enlarges the picture for the partially-sighted) and an Optacon
which is a reading machine.

Visitors can try out many of these aids, including a Braille
machine, mathematical equipment, embossed maps and
games, including embossed and large-print playing cards.

Educational provision
School parties are asked to arrange visits in advance.

Shop
Sunshine Shop open Mon to Fri, 10 a.m. – 4 p.m. sells gifts
from the Sunshine fund catalogue and articles made by blind
people.

Disabled
Toilets available.

ROYAL NATIONAL ROSE SOCIETY GARDENS

Chiswell Green Lane, St Albans, Herts AL2 3NR
Tel: (St Albans) 0727 50461

British Rail: St Albans City

Open
June 8 to Sept 29 9 a.m. – 5 p.m. Mon to Sat; 10 a.m. – 6 p.m.
Sun.
Closed Oct to May.

Admission charges
Children   (accompanied and under 16) free.
Adults   £1.20.
Parties   £1 per person.
School Parties   30p per person.

The **Royal National Rose Society Gardens** have historical,
species and modern roses – in all some 30,000 plants in 12
acres of gardens. Of special interest are the Trial Grounds
where the future 'Greats' of the rose world are to be found.

Refreshments
Cafeteria open 10.30 a.m. – 4.30 p.m. Mon to Sat and 12 noon –
5.30 p.m. Sun.

Shop
Shop open 9 a.m. – 5 p.m. Mon to Sat and 10 a.m. – 6 p.m. Sun.
Shop sells gifts and souvenirs.

Disabled
Wheelchairs available at the gate (free but best to reserve
beforehand). Full toilet facilities.

ROYAL SOCIETY OF PAINTERS IN WATERCOLOURS

(See Bankside Gallery.)

RSPB RYE HOUSE MARSH RESERVE

Rye House Information Centre, Rye Road, Hoddesdon, Herts
Tel: (Hoddesdon) 0992 460031

British Rail: Rye House

Open
10 a.m. – 4 p.m. Sat and Sun.
Closed weekdays, when school parties may visit by arrangement.

Admission charges
Free at weekends (self-guiding). Weekday parties 75p per person per half day for courses.

RSPB Rye House Marsh Reserve has several observation hides overlooking the riverside marsh. In winter, snipe, teal, kingfisher and water rail can be seen and in summer, reed and sedge warblers. Marsh plants include marsh marigold, ragged robin, water forget-me-not and comfrey. The information centre has leaflets and publications and display boards on the Reserve.

Educational provision
Lecture Room, worksheets, teachers' guides, binoculars and observation hides available.

Disabled
One hide with space for 2 to 4 wheelchairs. Toilets adjacent to site.

ST ALBANS CITY MUSEUM

Hatfield Road, St Albans, Herts AL1 3RR
Tel: (St Albans) 0727 56679

British Rail: St Albans

Open

10 a.m. – 5 p.m. Mon to Sat.
Closed Sun, Christmas Day, Boxing Day and all other Public
holidays.

Admission charges

Free.

The **St Albans City Museum** has collections of local and
natural history and a fine collection of craft tools displayed in
reconstructed workshops. There are mini dioramas of
Hertfordshire habitats and period rooms. The Salaman
collection of craft tools is of national importance and has
implements used by wheelwrights, carpenters and
shipwrights. The workshops are a wheelwright's, saw pit and a
cooper's shop. The regional geological collection has a very
good butterfly collection.

Educational provision

Gallery talks by the Keeper of Local History and the Keeper of
Natural History can be arranged. Assistance with projects is
available and handling sessions for school pupils can be
organised.

Shop

Shop open during museum times sells books, posters,
postcards, jewellery, pens and pencils.

ST BARTHOLOMEW THE GREAT

57 West Smithfield, London EC1
(Letters to Church House, Cloth Fair, London EC1A 7JQ)
Tel: 01-606 1575

Underground: Barbican and St Paul's

Open

Winter   8.30 a.m. (10.30 Tues) – 4 p.m. Mon to Sun.
Summer   8.30 a.m. (10.30 Tues) – 5 p.m. Mon to Sun.
Never closed.

Admission charges
Free.

St Bartholomew The Great is a fine Norman church founded in 1123, by Rahere, who is buried here. The church has a wonderful history. There are marvellous Roman arches; where the All Soul's Chapel is now there was a forge, and the cloister was used as a stable to raise funds for rebuilding after Henry VIII's time. The Oriel window is Bolton's window in the triforium where he himself lived and it has his signature at the bottom – a bolt and a ton. The cloister in the East Wing has roof springing with bosses with coats of arms and masonry in the 15th century style done in 1902-22. Hogarth was baptised here and Benjamin Franklin was working here as a printer.

There are fully choral services every Sunday at 11 a.m. and 6.30 p.m.

Special events
On Good Friday there is the distribution of the Butterworth Charity. Nowadays, instead of giving a few pence to the widows of the Parish, hot cross buns are distributed to the children.

Shop
Bookstall sells postcards.

Disabled
Wheelchair access.

ST BRIDE'S CHURCH AND CRYPT MUSEUM

St Bride's Rectory, Fleet Street, London EC4Y 8AU
Tel: 01-353 1301

Underground: Blackfriars

Open
9 a.m. – 5 p.m. Daily. Holy Communion celebrated at 8.30 a.m. Mon to Fri.
Never closed.

Admission charges
Free.

The present **St Bride's Church**, named after the Celtic saint
St Bridget of Kildare, is the eighth church on this site. Of the
last three churches, the sixth was destroyed in the Great Fire of
London in 1666, to be rebuilt by Christopher Wren whose
design for the steeple inspired a local baker in the 18th century
to copy it for a wedding cake. His cake caught on, and it is now
the popular form. The church was devasted in the Second
World War but fortunately Wren's plans were saved, and a
replica was built and rededicated in 1957.

The Crypt Museum follows the history of the church, with
remains of a Roman pavement, an account of the 6th century
Celtic church, medieval relics, 14th century chapel and
contemporary engravings of the Great Plague and Great Fire.
There are WCs available.

Educational provision
A booklet 'St Bride's Church Fleet Street in the City of
London' on sale, price 50p.

Shop
Book table sells pamphlets and religious newspapers.

Disabled
No special facilities but wheelchairs may come in to the
church via the West Door where there are no steps. No steps in
toilets.

ST JOHN'S GATE

(See Museum of the Order of St John.)

ST KATHARINE'S DOCK

(See Historic Ship Collection.)

ST MARY MAGDELENE NATURE RESERVE INTERPRETATIVE CENTRE MUSEUM

Norman Road, East Ham, London E6
Tel: 01-470 4525

Underground: East Ham

Open
Nature Reserve   9 a.m. – 5 p.m. Mon to Fri; 2 – 5 p.m. Sat and Sun.
Interpretative Centre   2 – 5 p.m. Tues, Thurs, Sat and Sun.
School Parties
by arrangement.
Closed Bank and Public holidays.

Admission charges
Free.

The **St Mary Magdalene Interpretative Centre Museum** has a small display designed to interpret what is to be seen in the Nature Reserve. This is based on its overall ecology – simple food chains and food webs shown at a school pupil's level of interpretation. Staff are on hand to answer questions and to provide further, and more specific information. An outside panelled display can be seen when the Centre is closed.

The Nature Reserve itself is an unspoiled urban wilderness, populated with foxes, pheasants, tawney owls, kestrels, weasels, rabbits, numerous birds and insects and 18 different kinds of butterflies. These are all the natural inhabitants, nothing has been introduced.

Educational provision
Worksheets, teachers' guides and lecture room are all available on request. Contact Extension Services Section (tel: 01-534 0276).

Shop
Shop open during visiting hours selling nature trail guides and books.

ST PAUL'S CATHEDRAL

St Paul's Churchyard, London EC4M 8AD
Tel: 01-248 2705

Underground: St Paul's

Open

Summer   10 a.m. – 4.15 p.m. Daily.
Winter   10 a.m. – 3.15 p.m. Daily.
Never closed.
Ambulatory, Crypt and Galleries are open on weekdays at the
above times, and Sat at 11 a.m.

Admission charges

Ambulatory
Children   free.
Adults   40p.
Party rate   (10 or more)   20p per person.
Crypt
Children   30p.
Adults   70p.
Party rate   50p per person.
Galleries
Children   35p.
Adults   75p.
Party rate   55p per person.
School Parties
Must be pre-booked through the registrar. Church floor and
Ambulatory free; Crypt 20p; Galleries 25p.
Guiding fee for tour parties 50p per person.

St Paul's Cathedral was the fifth to be built upon the summit
of Ludgate Hill where a cathedral has stood for thirteen and a
half centuries. Sir Christopher Wren's greatest Renaissance
church rises majestically over the City, a landmark built to
replace the previous cathedral which was totally destroyed in
the Great Fire of 1666.

The foundation stone for Wren's cathedral was laid on
21 June 1675 and the building completed by the end of that

century so Wren saw his masterpiece completed during his lifetime.

The design is based on the traditional Latin cross with a domed crossing between nave and choir. The dome's windows and pilasters have niches at intervals, accomodating statues. Above are the Thornhill frescoes, depicting the life of St Paul.

Amongst the superb features of the church are the ironwork by Jean Tijou, mosaics by Sir William Richmond, wood carvings by Grinling Gibbons, Roll of Honour in the American Memorial Chapel, and Holman Hunt's *The Light of the World*. Admiral Lord Nelson and Wren himself are among these buried here, with memorials to Wellington, Sir Joshua Reynolds, Turner, Lord Cornwallis, Kitchener, Lord Melbourne, Captain Scott and the members of his expedition who failed to return from the South Pole in 1912. The sculpture of John Donne, St Paul's most famous Dean, is the only complete statue to have survived the Great Fire.

Throughout the day there are prayers and services in the cathedral, which has its own choir and choir school.

Educational provision
Guides are available on request and a tape/slide show is given in the Crypt every half-hour.

Shop
Shop open 10 a.m. – 4 p.m. sells guidebooks, postcards, records, slides and souvenirs.

Disabled
Wheelchair lift to church floor on application to a Verger.

SALVATION ARMY STORY MUSEUM

117-121 Judd Street, Kings Cross, London WC1H 9NN
Tel: 01-387 1656 extension 14

Underground: Kings Cross
British Rail: Kings Cross

Open
9.30 a.m. – 3.30 p.m. weekdays; Sat open by appointment only.
Closed Sun and Bank holidays.

Admission charges
Free.

The **Salvation Army Story Museum** tells the story of the Army from its foundation in 1865 by William Booth to the present day by means of pictures, maps, photographs, priceless items, slides and films.

On display are the communion sets used by William Booth as a Methodist Minister, and during the Mission period of the organisation. Also on view are Booth's Love Feast Cup, and prison uniforms which Salvation Army members were forced to wear in gaol.

Educational provision
Free quiz sheets, a selection of free leaflets, students' and teachers' packs are available.

Films and slide lectures can be arranged if advance notice is given.

Refreshments
Cafeteria open during museum hours.

Shop
Shop open 9.30 a.m. – 4.30 p.m. selling books, records and tapes.

SAMBOURNE HOUSE

(See Linley Sambourne House.)

SCIENCE MUSEUM

Exhibition Road, South Kensington, London SW7 2OD
Tel: 01-589 3456

Underground: South Kensington

Open
10 a.m. – 6 p.m. Mon to Sat; 2.30 – 6 p.m. Sun.
Closed 24, 25, 26 Dec, 1 Jan, Good Friday and May Day.

Admission charges
Free.

The **Science Museum** has displays covering all forms of
science and technology, pure science, medicine, engineering
and industry. About 50,000 items have been collected since
the museum opened in 1857 and about 1,000 more are added
each year. In addition 200,000 items of medical history have
recently been transferred by the Wellcome Museum which are
now housed here. These are not only big and special things
like airliners, atom-smashers, printing presses and spacecraft,
but also small and homely items – ball point pens, baby-
buggies and zip-fasteners. The Curators build collections
which are as representative as possible without gaps and
without duplication. The collections show the appliance of
science to everyday life, they conserve our scientific heritage,
and are also used for research. Among the exhibits are a model
of the Apollo II lunar module, Puffing Billy train, and an
operating amateur radio station. The Children's Gallery in the
basement has working models.

Educational provision
The schools' entrance is in Imperial College Road. Parties
should pre-book and avoid March, June and July. The
Museum runs teachers' courses and presents audio-visual
programmes and lectures for school-children. Worksheets,
study packs and activity sheets cover a number of subjects and
ages. A lunchroom is available by advance booking only.

Refreshments
Small tea bar open daily until 5 p.m.

Shop
Museum shop open 11 a.m. – 5.45 p.m. Mon and Tues,
10 a.m. – 5.45 p.m. Wed to Sat and 2.30 – 5.45 p.m. Sun sells
postcards, posters, publications, books, slides and souvenirs.

Disabled
There is a ramp to the first floor and lifts to all floors, but
special arrangements must be made for visits to the basement,
which includes the Children's Gallery. Toilets also available.

SERPENTINE GALLERY

Kensington Gardens, London W2 3XA
Tel: 01-402 6075 or 01-723 9072

Underground: South Kensington and Lancaster Gate.

Open
Apr – Oct   10 a.m. – 6 p.m. Daily.
Nov – Mar   10 a.m. – dusk Daily.
Closed Christmas Eve, Christmas Day, Boxing Day and
New Year's Day.

Admission charges
Free.

The **Serpentine Gallery** has changing monthly exhibitions of
contemporary painting, drawing, sculpture and photographs.

Shop
Shop open during gallery hours selling cards, posters,
catalogues and books.

Disabled
No special facilities but the gallery is all on one level.

SEWAGE TREATMENT WORKS

(See Thames Water Sewage Treatment Works and Pumping Stations.)

SHAW'S CORNER (National Trust)

Ayot St Lawrence, Welwyn, Herts
Tel: (Stevenage) 0438 820307

British Rail: Welwyn Garden City
Note: this is 6 miles from Shaw's Corner and a taxi must be taken as there is no public transport

---

Open
Apr – end of Oct   2 – 6 p.m. Mon to Thurs; 12 noon – 6 p.m. Sun and Bank holiday Mon.
Pre-booked groups
Mar – to end Nov   11 a.m. – 6 p.m. Sun to Thurs.
Closed Fri (including Good Fri), Sat and Dec to Feb.

Admission charges
Free to members of the National Trust (join here).
Children   60p.
Adults   £1.20.
Schools should take corporate membership giving free admission to all NT properties. Otherwise no reduction for parties except by written arrangement with the Custodian.

Shaw's Corner, George Bernard Shaw's home, has been left as it was when he died here in 1950. Here is his study, dining room, drawing room, hall, garden and writing hut. The house is an example of a middle-class home of the first part of this century. Shaw's hats still hang in the hall, his pens, dictionaries and typewriter are on his desk and many of his personal treasures can be seen.

Educational provision
A talk on Bernard Shaw's life here can sometimes be given to

pre-booked school or further education groups. The visit will be rewarding to those who already have some appreciation of Shaw and his challenging views on the theatre, politics and literature. School visits will benefit by a prior discussion between teacher and Custodian.

Shop
Postcards and guides are on sale.

Disabled
Wheelchairs can be accommodated but this is best on weekdays rather than Sundays or Bank holidays.

SIR JOHN SOANE'S MUSEUM

13 Lincoln's Inn Fields, London WC2
Tel: 01-405 2107

Underground: Holborn

Open
10 a.m. – 5 p.m. Tues to Sat.
Closed Sun and Mon and Bank and Public holidays.

Admission charges
Free.

Sir John Soane's Museum is the house and library of Sir John Soane who was Professor of Architecture at the Royal Academy and the architect of the Bank of England. He left his house and collections to the nation to remain untouched from the day he died in 1837. He collected and set out fragments and plaster casts of classical architecture of all periods, and assembled them in a way designed to fire the imagination of architects and those interested. In this way he sought to conjure up the 'poetry of architecture'. There is a marvellous collection of architectural drawings which can be consulted. Other major exhibits include very important Hogarth prints (including the *Rake's Progress*), and an Egyptian sarcophagus which was made from a single piece of alabaster.

Educational provision
A guided tour is given at 2.30 p.m. on Sat and an introductory talk is available to parties on request (contact the Curator).

Shop
Sales desk sells postcards, slides and guide books.

SOUTHEND FARM

Southend Lane, Waltham Abbey, Essex EN9 3SE
Tel: (Lea Valley) 0992 715283/716480

Underground: Epping

Open
Mar – Nov   Mon to Fri by appointment.
Closed Sat and Sun and Dec to Feb.

Admission charges
£28 per visit for up to 45 children.
50p per extra child, accompanying adults free.

Southend Farm is open for visits by groups of people. It is a mixed farm with sheep, wildfowl, turkeys, trout lakes, beef and dairy cows, chickens and ducks. All the animals are people-trained, and every visitor has the opportunity to milk a cow by hand, There is a guided tour round the farm, geared to the overall age of the children. As well as educational visitors, clubs and groups are encouraged to come in the afternoons or evenings when teas and dinners are served – prices on application.

Shop
Craft centre open for adult visitors only.

Disabled
There is access to most parts of the farm.

SOUTHSIDE HOUSE

3 Woodhayes Road, Wimbledon, London SW19 4RJ
Tel: 01-946 7643

Underground: Wimbledon
British Rail: Wimbledon

Open
Oct 1 – Mar 31   2 – 5 p.m. Tues, Thurs, Fri; Guided tours at
2, 3, 4 and 5 p.m.
Closed Mon, Wed, Sat, Sun and from Apr to Sept.

Admission charges
Children   (accompanied by adult)   50p.
Adults   £1.
Student   50p.
School Parties
50p.

Southside House was built in the Dutch Baroque style in 1687
and is still a private residence. It is the former home of
Mrs Hilda Pennington-Mellor-Munthe, wife of the Swedish
doctor and philanthropist Axel Munthe, who wrote his
memoirs – *The Story of San Michele* – in this house. It
contains furniture of the 18th and 19th centuries, Queen Anne
Boleyn's vanity case, and Marie Antoinette's necklace.

Shop
Guidebook, price 30p, on sale on admission.

SOUTHWARK CATHEDRAL

London Bridge, London SE1
Tel: 01-407 2939

Underground: London Bridge

Open

8 a.m. – 6.30 p.m. Daily.
Never closed.

Admission charges

Free.

Southwark Cathedral, 1212, is the earliest Gothic church in
London, and has a fine 15th century choir, original wooden
roof bosses (which date back to the wooden roof in the Nave)
and Norman door. Southwark Cathedral is referred to as the
Cathedral of Common Man rather than the Cathedral of
Kings and Queens. Its monuments are to ordinary people, for
example the Humble family (city aldermen), the modern-day
saint and theologian – Lancelot Andrews who was the former
Bishop of Winchester and is now recognised in the Alternative
Services Prayer Book. Shakespeare's brother is buried in the
choir and there is a memorial to John Gower poet to Richard
III.

Shop

Bookstall open 11 a.m. – 4 p.m. sells a variety of books,
educational material and goods.

SPITALFIELDS FARM

**c/o Thomas Buxton School, Buxton Street,
London E1 5AR
Tel: 01-247 8762**

Underground: Aldgate East, Whitechapel and Shoreditch
British Rail: Liverpool Street

Open

10 a.m. – 5 p.m. Daily.
Never closed.

Admission charges

Free.

Spitalfields Farm consists of animal houses, a barn, stables, duckponds, paddocks, workshop, tackroom and the original allotments, on an acre of British Rail land. Livestock includes: geese, chickens, sheep, goats, bantams, Shetland ponies, donkeys, ducks and guinea fowl.

Visitors can help with the general farm work and, by arrangement, do spinning, weaving and go riding.

Educational provision

Worksheets are available on request with a classroom for up to 10 children. Please book when bringing a group.

Shop

Shop open during visiting hours sells woollen handicrafts, eggs, goats' milk, yoghurt and cheese.

Disabled

There are ramps and flat paths to every part of the farm providing wheelchair access.

SQUERRYES COURT

Westerham, Kent TN16 1SJ
Tel: 0959 62345

Road access only

Open

Mar 1 – Sept 30   2 – 6 p.m. Sun, Bank holiday Mon.
Apr 1 – Sept 30   2 – 6 p.m. Sun, Wed, Sat, Bank holiday Mon.
(last entry 5.30 p.m.). Parties any day except Sun.
Closed Nov to Feb; Mon, Tues, Thurs, Fri and Mon – Sat in Mar.

Admission charges

Children   (under 14) 70p.
Adults   £1.40.
School Parties
60p each for under 15s. *Adults* £1.20.

Squerryes Court, built in 1681, is a typical William and Mary period manor house. The Wardes, whose family home it has been for over 250 years, still live in the house. It contains a very fine collection from the Dutch school – Vandyck, Rubens and Ruisdael, and also of English portrait painters of the 18th and 19th centuries including Wootton, Tomney, Opie and Stubbs. There are tapestries, embroidery, furniture and porcelain.

The grounds, landscaped in the 18th century, have many beautiful trees, rhododendrons, and azaleas. There are lovely formal gardens and a lake.

Refreshments
The Tea Room is open at weekends 3 – 5 p.m. can be booked at other times for parties.

STEPPING STONES FARM

Stepney Way, London E1
Tel: 01-790 8204 (let the phone ring a long time)

Underground: Stepney Green
British Rail: Stepney East

Open
9.30 a.m. – 1 p.m. and 2 – 6 p.m. Tues to Sun.
Closed Mon.

Admission charges
Free.

Stepping Stones Farm is a working farm with a complete range of farm animals – cattle, sheep, pigs, goats, poultry and rabbits. Depending on the time of day, visitors can see all the aspects of farming, including feeding and milking. When not involved in the urgent jobs, the staff are on hand to answer questions, and discuss the various aspects of farming. Individuals are welcome at any time during opening hours.

Individuals and small groups of up to 10 can help out with the animals and odd jobs around the farm.

Special events
Throughout the summer many events are organised, often at the last minute. There are games and inflatables on most weekends.

Educational provision
There is a small classroom (maximum 15 children) and a teachers' pack with worksheet will be available soon. Teachers can also obtain a pack from the East London Teachers' Centre, English Street, London E2. The management stress that they believe that most learning is through talking and helping and playing on the farm. This is an informal and flexible place, and staff will do their very best to cater for the needs of their visitors.

Refreshments
Teas are sometimes available.

Disabled
The whole farm is easily accessible for the disabled, being built round an old road; other paths are ramped. There is a toilet block for the disabled and access for special vehicles.

STOCK EXCHANGE

Corner of Old Broad Street and Threadneedle Street, London EC2N 1HP
Tel: 01-588 2355

Underground: Bank and Cannon Street

Open
9.45 a.m. – 3.15 p.m. (last admission 3 pm.) Weekdays.
Booking in advance is *strongly* advised.
Closed weekends, Christmas Eve, Christmas Day, Boxing Day, New Year's Eve and Bank holidays.

Admission charges
Free.

The **Stock Exchange** has a Visitors' Gallery from which the trading floor can be seen in action. A talk by one of the guides describes the workings of the Stock Exchange, and this is followed by a film show entitled *My Word Is My Bond* – the Stock Exchange motto. Each month there is a different exhibition in the Gallery.

A 'City Trail' is available from the shop in the Visitors' Gallery entrance.

Educational provision
Booklets and literature on the workings of the Stock Exchange are available.

Shop
Shop open 9.45 a.m. – 3.15 p.m. sells souvenirs, educational books on the Stock Exchange, postcards and slides.

Disabled
There are facilities for the disabled in limited numbers.

SUFFOLK COLLECTION

(See Rangers House.)

SURREY DOCKS FARM

**Commercial Dock Passage, off Gulliver Street, Rotherhithe, London SE16
Tel: 01-231 1010**

Underground: Surrey Docks

Open

School term time
3.30 – 5 p.m. Tues to Fri; 10 a.m. – 5 p.m. Sat and Sun.
Closed Mon.
School holidays
10 a.m. – 5 p.m. Tues to Thurs, Sat and Sun.
Closed Mon and Fri.

Admission charges
Free.

Surrey Docks Farm is situated on the banks of the Thames in the middle of the ever changing Docklands, and its situation is unique in this respect. The various farm animals include goats, pigs, chickens, ducks, donkeys, geese, dogs, bees, sheep and others.

Visitors can wander freely around the farm and can help in all aspects of the farm's work in looking after the animals.

Educational provision
A full-time ILEA teacher is seconded to the farm which has a classroom. School visits during term-time can be arranged via Richard Mudge at the farm.

Shop
Shop open during visiting times sells goat's milk, goat's cheese, eggs, yoghurt, honey, compost and sawdust.

Disabled
The disabled have access to the field though this can be uneven and bumpy sometimes. There are no special toilet facilities.

SYON HOUSE

Syon Park, Brentford, Middlesex TW8 8JF
Tel: 01-560 0881-3

Underground: Gunnersbury
British Rail: Kew Bridge

Open

Apr 1 – Sept 29   12 noon – 5 p.m. (last ticket 4.15 p.m.) Sun to Thurs.

Oct   12 noon – 5 p.m. Sun only.

Closed Nov to Mar.

Admission charges

House only

Children   (under 17)   50p.

Adults   85p.

OAP   50p.

Combined House and Gardens

Children   (under 17)   70p.

Adults   £1.50.

OAP   70p.

School Parties

House only 40p, House and Garden 60p per person.

Syon House is a seat of the Duke of Northumberland, which Robert Adam transformed in his own style to the requirements of the then Earl of Northumberland, with surrounding gardens originally landscaped by Capability Brown. In 55 acres of parkland are the gardens, the great conservatory (containing an aviary and an aquarium), a six-acre rose garden and one of the most comprehensive horticultural garden centres in the country.

All party bookings should be made at least one week in advance.

Refreshments

Cafeteria in the park open 9.30 a.m. – 4.30 p.m. and Restaurant open 12 a.m. – 3 p.m. and 6.30 – 10 p.m.

Shop

Souvenir shop sells gifts and memorabilia.

TATE GALLERY

Millbank, London SW1P 4RG
Tel: 01-821 1313, recorded information 01-821 7128

Underground: Pimlico

Open
10 a.m. – 5.50 p.m. Mon to Sat; 2 – 5.50 p.m. Sun.
Closed Christmas Eve, Christmas Day, Boxing Day,
New Year's Day, Good Friday, May Day.

Admission charges
None to the permanent collection. Charges are made for
special exhibitions.

The **Tate Gallery** houses the National Collection of British
Art and the National Collection of Modern Art. The British
Collection consists of works from the 16th century up to about
1900 with a particularly strong showing of: Hogarth, William
Blake, Stubbs, Constable and J M W Turner. The
Pre-Raphaelites are also especially well-represented.

The Modern Collection incorporates the most extensive
survey of British art of its period in any public collection,
including selected examples of very recent art. The
development of modern art abroad is traced from
Impressionism through Cezanne, Gauguin, Van Gogh,
Bonnard, Matisse, Picasso (including one of his masterpieces
The Three Dancers), Braque, Futurism, Dada and Surrealism
to postwar European and American art including Abstract
Expressionism, Pop, Minimal and Conceptual art.

The Print Collection is part of the Modern Collection and it
seeks to represent the outstanding artists of the period who
have made prints an importrant part of their work. It thus
reflects the breadth of tendencies and idioms of the period,
from Joseph Beuys to Georg Baselitz, from Jasper Johns to Sol
Leitt or from Henry Moore to Barry Flanagan.

Special exhibitions
For details of future exhibitions, phone the Gallery.

Educational provision
The Education Department arranges: lectures, guided tours, film, slide and video programmes, courses for teachers, and worksheets and questionnaires for all ages. Teachers are asked to make contact with the department at least three weeks in advance, (six weeks if talk required).

Refreshments
Restaurant open 12 noon – 3 p.m. Mon to Sat. Coffee Shop open 10.30 a.m. – 5 .30 p.m. Mon to Sat; 2 – 5.15 p.m. Sun.

Shop
Shop open 10 a.m. – 5.30 p.m. Mon to Sat and 2 – 5.30 p.m. Sun selling books, prints, postcards, greetings cards and slides.

Disabled
Wheelchairs are provided at the Atterbury Street entrance where there is a ramp and lift giving access to the main floor – prior notice is requested. If booked in advance special tours can be arranged for disabled groups and there is an induction loop system in the Lecture Room.

TELECOM TECHNOLOGY SHOWCASE

135 Queen Victoria Street, London EC4V 4AT
Tel: 01-248 7444

Underground: Blackfriars

Open
10 a.m. – 5 p.m. Mon to Fri and the day of the Lord Mayor's Show.
Closed weekends and bank holidays.

Admission charges
Free.

The **Telecom Technology Showcase** is a unique exhibition which ranges over 200 years of progress from the earliest telegraph systems to modern examples of information technology, through a series of displays, videos and working models.

Early telegraphs and switchboards, the Rothschild's ivory and gilt telephones, an Edwardian cable-carried entertainment service, Prestel, telex, slow-scan TV, digital facsimile, satellite communications, and System X are all on show. In 1985 a new network area with talking model will be open.

Educational provision
Project sheets, lecture theatre and videos available.

Shop
Shop open during visiting hours sells educational books, posters, postcards and souvenirs.

THAMES BARRIER VISITORS' CENTRE

1 Unity Way, Woolwich, London SE18 5NJ
Tel: 01-854 1373

British Rail: Charlton (then 14 minutes walk)

Open
Summer   10.30 a.m. – 6 p.m. Daily.
Winter   10.30 a.m. – 5 p.m. Daily.
Closed Christmas Day and Boxing Day.

Admission charges
Free.

The **Thames Barrier** is one of the world's great engineering achievements. At the Visitors' Centre there is an exhibition with a working model and a 7 minute film showing the various stages of construction of the Barrier. There is also a presentation using film, slides and commentary to describe the history of London's flood problem, and the solution with the construction of the Barrier.

There are 20 minute boat trips around the Barrier with running commentary. (Party rates available – contact Sargent Bros Ltd, Unity House, Unity Way, Woolwich SE18 5NL, tel: 01-854 5555).

On certain days visitors can see the Barrier fully closed.

Educational provision
An educational pack for all levels is available. Classroom/ lecture room facilities will be available soon.

Refreshments
Cafeteria open during visiting hours (Bookings on 01-854 9961). Special packed lunches for children by arrangement.

Shop
Shop open during visiting hours sells souvenirs of the Barrier and the Thames.

Disabled
The disabled have access through the Centre via ramps and a lift from the car park to the Embankment defences of the river.

THAMES WATER RESERVOIRS

Thames Water, New River Head, Rosebery Avenue, London EC1R 4TP
Tel: 01-837 3300

Open
Times of access vary. Phone 01-837 3300 to check times prior to visiting site.

Admission charges

Permits must be obtained in advance from the above address.
Permit holders must be 16 or over.
Children above age of 8 are allowed in free but they must be
accompanied by a permit holder.
For parties of visitors the minimum age is 11 years.

Amongst other recreational activities, **Thames Water** allows
bird-watching at several of its reservoirs as follows:

Barn Elms, Merthyr Terrace, Barnes, London SW13
Underground: Hammersmith
**Kempton Park West, Sunbury Way, Hanworth,
Middlesex**
British Rail: Sunbury
**Queen Mary Reservoir, Ashford Road, Ashford,
Middlesex**
British Rail: Ashford or Sunbury
**Staines North and South, Staines, Middlesex (no permit
needed)**
British Rail: Staines
Walthamstow, Ferry Lane, Tottenham, London N17
Underground and British Rail: Tottenham Hale and
Waltham Cross
**Walton Reservoirs, Hurst Road, Walton-on-Thames,
Surrey**
British Rail: Walton-on-Thames

THAMES WATER-SEWAGE TREATMENT
WORKS AND PUMPING STATIONS

**Abbey Mill Sewage Pumping Station, Abbey Lane,
London E15**
Tel: 01-534 6717
Beckton Works, Jenkins Lane, Barking, Essex
Tel: 01-591 3911
Beddington Works, Beddington Lane, Croydon CR0 4TH
Tel: 01-689 0171
British Rail: Beddington Lane

Crossness Works, Belvedere Road, Abbey Wood,
London SE2
Tel: 01-310 1116
Deephams Works, Picketts Lock Lane, Edmonton,
London N9
Tel: 01-807 0121
British Rail: Lower Edmonton
Hogsmill Works, Lower March Lane, Kingston-upon-
Thames KT1 3BW
Tel: 01-399 5231
British Rail: Berrylands
Mogden Works, Mogden Lane, Isleworth, Middlesex
Tel: 01-560 3235
British Rail: Isleworth
Western Sewage Pumping Station, 124 Grosvenor Road,
London SW1
Tel: 01-730 5393

Open
By arrangement only. Organised groups will be given guided
tours. All visits must be arranged in advance.

Admission charges
Free.

Arrangements for visits must be made directly with the works
concerned. Please note that these establishments are
operational works, and visits may be subject to cancellation
for operational reasons. Those works where a British Rail
station is not indicated are not readily accessible by public
transport and visitors will have to provide their own transport.

THAMES WATER – WATER TREATMENT WORKS

Thames Water, New River Head, Rosebery Avenue,
London EC1R 4TP
Tel: 01-837 3300

Open
By arrangement only. Organised groups will be given guided tours. All visits must be arranged in advance.

Admission charges
Free.

Thames Water has three Works which may be visited by groups of students and others, at the following sites:

Ashford Common Works, Staines Road West, Ashford, Middlesex.
Coppermills Works, Coppermill Lane, Walthamstow, London E17.
Hampton Works, Upper Sunbury Road, Hampton, Middlesex.

Arrangements to visit these sites must be made with Thames Water at their Rosebery Avenue address.

THOMAS CORAM FOUNDATION
(See Foundling Hospital AA Gallery and Museum.)

TILBURY FORT
Tilbury, Essex
Tel: 03752 3285

British Rail: Tilbury Town

Open
Mar 15 – Oct 15   9.30 a.m. – 6.30 p.m. Mon to Sat;
2 – 6.30 p.m. Sun.
Oct 16 – Mar 14   9.30 a.m. – 4.30 p.m. Mon to Sat;
2 – 4 p.m. Sun.
Closed Daily from 1 – 2 p.m. and Christmas Eve, Christmas Day, Boxing Day and New Year's Day.

240

Admission charges
Children (under 16) 30p.
Adults 60p.
OAP and UB40 45p.
Free admission to monuments is granted to parties of students
receiving full-time education. Form AM 24 gives details and is
available from Area Office, English Heritage, Thames House
North, Millbank, London SW1P 4QJ (tel: 01-211 8828). Free
admission is not available from April 1 to September 30.

Tilbury Fort was commissioned by Charles II after an
audacious raid up the Thames by the Dutch in 1667. It took 13
years to build but never saw the action for which it was
designed. In the First World War a German Zeppelin was
gunned down from the parade ground. Entry is now from the
landward side across two restored bridges.

Educational provision
An education room can be booked in advance and details of
free educational resources can be obtained from Education
Service, English Heritage, Room 3/25, 15-17 Great
Marlborough Street, London W1V 1AF (tel: 01-734 6010
extension 810).

Shop
Ticket kiosk sells books, guides and souvenirs.

Disabled
Parking facilities. Fort square and magazines are the only parts
accessible.

TOPOLSKI'S MEMOIR OF THE CENTURY

**Hungerford Viaduct Arches, Concert Hall Approach,
South Bank Arts Centre, London SE1.
Tel: 01-928 3405** (the artist)

Underground: Waterloo

Open
5 – 8 p.m. Mon to Sat.
Closed Sun.

Adm..sion charges
Free.

Feliks Topolski has travelled the world, recording in his paintings and drawings the conflicts of the 20th century – Europe in the twenties and thirties, the Second World War, and wherever social change is afoot. Topolski has also turned his eye to satirising British institutions and youth cults.

The GLC has cleared and re-equipped the two arches beneath Hungerford Bridge where Topolski's panoramic painting, his 'Memoir of the Century', is dramatically displayed and he is still working on it. There are sculptures, a film of his Coronation Panorama in Buckingham Palace, and slide projections of 80 drawings of the Blitz.

From 5 – 8 p.m. on Fridays, Topolski's studio in Arch 158 is open to the public. In a warm and welcoming atmosphere visitors can view other works and speak to the artist who is always ready to answer questions.

Educational provision
Two free descriptive pamphlets are available and the artist's volumes on the chronicle can be examined.

Shop
Shop open during visiting hours sells prints.

TOWER BRIDGE

London SE1 2UP
Tel: 01-407 0922, 01-403 3761/5386

Underground: Tower Hill

Open
Apr 1 – Oct 31   10 a.m. – 6.30 p.m. Daily.
Nov 1 – Mar 31   10 a.m. – 4 p.m. Daily.

Closed Christmas Eve, Christmas Day, Boxing Day, New Year's Day and Good Friday.

Admission charges
Children (under 16) £1.
Adults £2.
OAP £1.
School Parties
One in 10 free.

Tower Bridge and its Walkways were opened in 1982. In the main towers are drawings of the bridge structure, and machinery displays about the history and building of the bridge. From the overhead walkways there are marvellous views up and down the Thames. Under the South Approach is the original steam pumping plant, some of which is still working. A video shows the opening of the bascules and an animated diagram shows how it used to operate.

Shop
Shop opens the same times as the Bridge, sells many items at all price ranges, including books and brochures.

Disabled
There are special toilet facilities, lifts and a wheelchair ramp on the high walkways.

TOWER OF LONDON

London EC3N 4AB
Tel: 01-709 0765 extension 247

Underground: Tower Hill

Open
Mar 1 – Oct 31 9.30 a.m. – 5.45 p.m. (last ticket 5 p.m.) Mon to Sat; 2 – 5.45 p.m. (last ticket 5 p.m.) Sun.
Nov – Feb 9.30 a.m. – 4.30 p.m. Mon to Sat (last ticket 4 p.m.).

Closed Sun from Nov – Feb, Christmas Eve, Christmas Day, Boxing Day, New Year's Day and Good Friday.

Admission charges
Mar – Oct
Children (5 – 15) £1.15.
Adults £3.
OAP £1.50.
Nov – Feb
Children (5 – 15) £1.15.
Adults £2.
OAP £1.
Note: children under the age of 10 must be accompanied by an adult..
School Parties
Sept – Apr free except Sat and Sun in Apr and Sept, and Bank holidays.
Note: Pupils must be over the age of 7.
Parties of 11 or more
10% reduction.
Yeoman Warders take tours throughout the day. The tour lasts about 1 hour and is not suitable for children under 10.

The **Tower of London** was first built by William the Conqueror in the 11th century to protect and control the city. At first it lay within the Roman city walls but it was enlarged in the 12th century, and added to in every century thereafter, so that it now covers 18 acres.

The White Tower is the oldest building and has been used both as a prison and for royal apartments. This Tower was used as a palace for 600 years up until James I in 1603.

At the same time, many executions took place on Tower Hill and the Tower Green, including those of Anne Boleyn, Katharine Howard, Lady Jane Grey and the Earl of Essex.

Beneath St Thomas' Tower, the Traitors' Gate was a landing-place for prisoners coming from trial at Westminster. Those who passed through include Sir Thomas More and Oliver Cromwell.

Its history of royal palace and place of execution is reflected in the exhibitions at the Tower – the crown jewels, dating from 17th century (jewels before that time were melted down by Oliver Cromwell), and the suits of armour and medieval weapons.

Educational provision
Sample worksheets can be supplied and teachers' courses are held from time to time. Talks, audio-visuals and activities in the Education Centre are integrated with work in the Tower to make up a full-day programme. Audio-visual presentations are available on a number of topics.

Refreshments
Self-service restaurant open 9.30 a.m. – 4.30 p.m. in winter, and 9.30 a.m. – 7 p.m. in summer, sells snacks and ice cream. Some kiosks are situated on the Wharf. Packed lunches may be eaten here.

Shop
Two shops open during visiting hours sell guide books, postcards, gifts and souvenirs.

Disabled
Few buildings are accessible by wheelchair – only the Oriental and Heralds Gallery, History Gallery and the Chapel Royal of St Peter.

TRADESCANT MUSEUM OF GARDEN HISTORY

St Mary-At-Lambeth, Lambeth Palace Road, London SE1 7JU
Tel: 01-261 1891

Underground: Waterloo
British Rail: Waterloo and Victoria

Open
Second Sun in Mar to first Sun in Dec   11 a.m. – 3 p.m. Mon to Fri; 10.30 a.m. – 5 p.m. Sun.
Closed second Sun in Dec – last Sun in Mar, and Sat.

The **Tradescant Museum of Garden History** is housed in the historic former church of St Mary-At-Lambeth which the Tradescant Trust rescued from demolition. The Trust conceived the idea of establishing here a living memorial to the glory of the English garden. Inspiration for this project derives from the fact that the two John Tradescants, father and son, gardeners successively to Charles I, who brought back from their travels in Europe and America many of the flowers, shrubs and trees we take for granted today, lie buried in the churchyard.

A 17th century garden, designed by the Marchioness of Salisbury, has been created in the churchyard, and contains many rare and interesting species.

In the church, photographs, books, porcelain and 16th – 19th century objects form the beginning of the Museum's collection which is to be expanded.

Special events 1985
For details of future events, phone the Museum.
Applications for special events should be made by letter, enclosing cheque or postal order where required, to: The Tradescant Trust, 7 The Little Boltons, London SW10 9LJ.

Educational provision
Talks can be given to educational groups if arranged beforehand.

Refreshments
Tea or coffee and biscuits can be provided if arranged beforehand.

Shop
Shop open during museum hours sells books, cards, gifts, sweets, slides, pot pourris and posters.

Disabled
There are ramps through the museum.

TUDOR BARN ART GALLERY

**Well Hall Pleasaunce, Well Hall Road, Eltham,
London SE9
Tel: 01-850 2340**

British Rail: Eltham Well Hall

Open
11 a.m. – 4.30 p.m. Sun and Wed to Fri; 11 a.m. – 12.30 p.m.
and 2.30 – 4.30 p.m. Mon and Tues.
Closed Sat; 12.30 a.m. – 2.30 p.m. Mon and Tues,
Christmas Day and Boxing Day.

Admission charges
Free.

The **Tudor Barn Art Gallery** is a 16th-century red brick barn
set in a large public park, which together form the remains of
the estate of Well Hall. The Barn is now owned by the London
Borough of Greenwich. The Gallery is on the first floor and
the ground floor is a public restaurant. It holds monthly art
exhibitions of paintings, drawings and prints by individual
artists and groups of artists from around the locality.

Special Events
For details of future exhibitions, phone the Gallery.

Refreshments
Restaurant open daily for coffee from 11 a.m. – 12 p.m. and
from 12p.m. – 2 p.m. for lunch. Family carvery service on
Sundays.

Disabled
Difficult access up a steep flight of stairs.

TYBURN CONVENT

8 Hyde Park Place, Bayswater Road, London W2 2LJ
Tel: 01-723 7262

Underground: Marble Arch

Open
By appointment only – times can be arranged to suit the group.
A guided tour of the crypt is given which is mainly of interest
to students of catholicism or history.

Admission charges
Free.

Tyburn Convent is a centre of devotion to the martyrs of the
Reformation period. Tyburn field, near Marble Arch, was a
place of public execution for all types of criminals and over
100 of the Reformation Martyrs were executed there on the
infamous triple gallows, between 1535 and 1681. The French
and Spanish embassies of the time made collections of relics
and these have been officially authenticated and are on display
in the crypt. Much research has been done into the lives and
deaths of the martyrs, now canonised as saints, and the guided
tour is most informative on historical and religious aspects.

UNIVERSITY COLLEGE DEPARTMENT OF EGYPTOLOGY

(See Petric Museum of Egyptian Archaeology.)

UPMINSTER SMOCK MILL

St Mary's Lane, Upminster, Essex
Tel: 04024 47535

Underground: Upminster
British Rail: Upminster

Open
Apr – Sept 2 – 5.30 p.m. Sat and Sun every third weekend in month.
Closed Oct – Mar.

Admission charges
Free.

Upminster Smock Mill was built around 1801 and is the only complete windmill left in the Greater London area. This is an authentic smock mill and everything inside is original. The windshaft was replaced in 1899 by the then miller with one from an old post mill in Essex. The roundel at its base is brick and the rest of the mill is timber with weatherboard cladding. Inside are the shaft, binds, grinding wheels, dust floor, stone floor, meal floor and storeroom (in the basement).

For safety purposes, visitors are taken round in groups of 10 to 20 by guides who explain thoroughly the workings of the mill and how the miller coped with the weather, and the risk of fire. From 1811 some coal-fired steam machinery was introduced and this is in the storeroom along with other remnants of the last miller's equipment – weighing machines and block and tackle.

Educational provision
The mill can be opened outside public visiting hours for school parties by arrangement.

Refreshments
Soft drinks on sale.

Shop
A sales desk sells postcards, books, badges, pens, pencils and leaflets.

UPMINSTER TITHE BARN AGRICULTURAL AND FOLK MUSEUM

Hall Lane, Upminster, Essex
Tel: 04024 47535

Underground: Upminster
British Rail: Upminster

Open
Apr – Oct 1.30 – 6 p.m. Sat and Sun, first weekend in each month.
Closed Nov – Mar.

Admission charges
Free.

The **Upminster Tithe Barn Agricultural and Folk Museum** building was built about 1450 and came to be known as a tithe barn although there is no evidence that tithes were collected in the area. The barn is a large timber-framed structure with a thatched roof and clad in a mixture of horizontal and vertical weatherboarding. It contains mainly agricultural and farming exhibits. Agricultural items include ploughs, seed drills, a Fordson tractor, a baler, reaper, and an Essex wagon. There are samples of locally made bricks and domestic items including lasts, etc. to do with cobbling. There are some foundry items – bellows and anvil – and amongst the samples of local objects is a bottle area with two samples from the local Hornchurch brewery and some from local dairies, now closed down.

Educational provision
Samples of worksheets are available for duplication and the barn can open for school parties at other times by arrangement.

Shop
Shop open during museum hours sells books, badges, pens, pencils, leaflets and postcards.

VALENCE HOUSE MUSEUM

Becontree Avenue, Dagenham, Essex RM8 3HT
Tel: 01-592 2211

Underground: Becontree
British Rail: Chadwell Heath

Open
By appointment only – 10 a.m. – 5 p.m. Mon to Fri.
Closed Sat, Sun and Bank holidays.

Admission charges
Free.

Valence House is the only manor house remaining in Dagenham, and it stands on an ancient moated site to the north of Valence Park. It houses a small local history museum which contains a collection of human artefacts from the locality: Stone Age and Bronze Age implements, Roman pottery, Anglo-Saxon ornaments and weapons. There are also numerous local topographical pictures and maps and the important collection of Fanshawe family portraits ranging from the time of Elizabeth I to Queen Victoria, and including works by important portraitists such as Marcus Gheeraedts and William Dobson. The present house dates mainly from the 17th century and is a listed building, having timber frame and still partially moated. The front entrance is flanked by a pair of whalebones brought from the ruins of Whalebone House, Chadwell Heath. The house has several rooms devoted to: maps (and engravings) of Essex, period furniture and panelling, pictures and prints of Hainault Forest, and Barking Town (this room is dominated by a fully-rigged model of a 19th century fishing smack).

Educational provision
A lecture room is available for visiting school parties and a catalogue can be sent (£1 plus postage).

Shop
Sales desk in the library open 9.30 a.m. – 7 p.m. (closing at 1 p.m. on Wednesdays) selling postcards, local publications.

Disabled
Although there are no lifts, most of the exhibits are on the first floor which is accessible for the disabled. Parking is available at the door by arrangement, but there are no special toilet facilities.

VAUXHALL CITY FARM

24 St Oswald's Place, London SE11 5JE
Tel: 01-582 4204

Underground: Vauxhall
British Rail: Vauxhall

Open
10.30. a.m. – 5 p.m. Tues, Wed, Thurs, Sat and Sun.
Closed Mon and Fri.

Admission charges
Free.

Vauxhall City Farm is a community project run by local people. The project began in 1977 on half an acre of derelict land originally owned by the GLC. At first, volunteers looked after a few animals. Gradually full-time workers have been employed and the stock increased so that it now includes: ponies, goats and kids, sheep and lambs, pigs and piglets, rabbits, guinea pigs, a donkey, a ferret, chickens (several breeds), ducks and geese. One of the most striking features of the farm is the mural which was finished by Rolf Harris who painted his cat in the corner.

The farm shears its own sheep, spins, weaves, dyes, and makes up the fleece into garments for fund-raising, and on Saturday morning a spinning club meets.

During school holidays many activities are organised for children.

Educational provision
Staff are available for talks to school groups and the following are available: school packs (£2) and worksheets (1p).

Refreshments
According to availability, tea and cakes can be provided at weekends.

Shop
The farm sells eggs and milk and sometimes cheese and yoghurt.

Disabled
Toilets available and paths are accessible to wheelchairs but rather uneven – everything can be seen from the paths.

VERULAMIUM ROMAN MUSEUM

St Michael's Street, St Albans, Herts AL3 4SW
Tel: (St Albans) 0727 59919

British Rail: St Albans

Open
Apr – Oct   10 a.m. – 5.30 p.m. Daily.
Nov – Mar   10 a.m. – 4 p.m. Daily.
Closed Christmas Day, Boxing Day and New Year's Day.

Admission charges
Free.

The **Verulamium Museum,** situated within the walls of the
Roman town, is noted for important collections of late Iron
Age and Roman material. It houses Roman mosaics, painted
wallplasters, glass, pottery, coins, and archaeological material
from other periods. The main gallery is devoted to the history
of the Roman town of Verulamium, and the side gallery to
various themes – kitchen, eating, death and burial. A few
minutes walk from the museum is the Roman Hypocaust, part
of the bath wing of a Roman town house preserved under a
modern cover-building. The Hypocaust features an under-
floor heating system and mosaic pavement.

Educational provision
The Keeper of Education is available for consultation and
teaching duties (though preference is given to Hertfordshire
schools when time is pressing). The Keeper welcomes
opportunities of discussing curricula needs, study projects and
general educational matters with teacher and lecturers.

Shop
Shop open 10 a.m. – 5.15 p.m. (summer) and 4 p.m. (winter)
sells postcards, publications, replicas, slides and models.

Disabled
Ramp into Museum entrance hall, double opening doors, and
toilets in Car Park. Museum all on one floor level with no
steps.

VESTRY HOUSE MUSEUM

Vestry Road, Walthamstow, London E17 9NH
Tel: 01-527 5544 extension 4391

Underground: Walthamstow Central

Open
10 a.m. – 5.30 p.m. Mon, Tues, Thurs and Fri; 10 a.m. – 1 p.m.
and 2 – 5.30 p.m. Wed and Sat.
Closed Sun, Christmas to New Year, Easter and Bank
holidays.

Admission charges
Free.
Advance notice required from all parties (whether needing
assistance or not) to avoid over-crowding.

The **Vestry House Museum** is housed in an 18th century
workhouse in the heart of Walthamstow village conservation
area. Galleries display costumes, Victorian and Edwardian
domestic life and a Victorian parlour. There are models of
Walthamstow in the past and archaeological relics. The
Bremer car, built 1892-4, and reputedly the first British car is
on show along with a Victorian Police cell. Children are
offered the chance to be locked in this cell.

In 1985 a new display of local crafts and industry will open.

Educational provision
Worksheets, introductory talks and a variety of slide shows are
available, also handling sessions, a limited number of replica
clothes and a small loans service – these facilities all need
booking.

Shop
Shop open during museum hours sells publications on local
history, postcards and posters.

Disabled
There is access to the lower floor for the disabled but this is
difficult.

VICTORIA AND ALBERT MUSEUM

Cromwell Road, London SW7
Tel: 01-589 6371 extension 429

Underground: South Kensington

Open
10 a.m. – 5.50 p.m. Mon to Thurs and Sat; 2 – 5.50 p.m. Sun.
Closed Fri, Christmas Eve, Christmas Day, Boxing Day,
New Year's Day and May Day.

Admission charges
Free.

The **Victoria and Albert Museum** has collections of fine and
decorative arts displayed primarily to show their historical
development and also as study material for specialists. The
works come from Britain, Europe, Islam, India and the Far
East and include paintings, drawings, prints, ceramics, textiles
and dress, sculpture, furniture, metalwork and photography.
The Museum has one of the finest collections of costumes and
also of musical instruments. It has the Raphael cartoons, and
the best collection of Italian Renaissance sculpture outside
Italy. The collections include works of art and design up to the
present day.

Educational provision
If four weeks notice is given, introductory talks on specific
subjects for groups of up to 20 can be given. Free
bibliographies of the Tudor, 17th century, Georgian and
Victorian periods are available.

Refreshments
Self-service restaurant open 10 – 11.45 a.m., 12 noon –
2.30 p.m. for lunch and 3 – 5 p.m. on Mon to Thurs and Sat;
2.30 – 5.30 p.m. on Sun.

Shop
Bookshop open 10 a.m. – 5.45 p.m. Mon to Thurs; 10 a.m. –
5.30 p.m. Sat; 2.30 – 5.30 p.m. Sun sells books, postcards,
slides, posters and small gifts.

Craftshop run by the Crafts Council with the same hours as the bookshop sells one-off pieces of work by leading craftspeople who are usually represented in the Museum's contemporary collections – including ceramics, glass, wood, jewellery, metalwork and textiles.

Disabled
Toilets, ramps and lifts. The whole museum is accessible by wheelchair except the Lecture Theatre.

WALLACE COLLECTION

Hertford House, Manchester Square, London W1M 6BN
Tel: 01-935 0687

Underground: Bond Street and Baker Street

Open
10 a.m. – 5 p.m. Mon to Sat; 2 – 5 p.m. Sun.
Closed Christmas Eve, Christmas Day, Boxing Day, New Year's Day, Good Friday and May Day.

Admission charges
Free.

The **Wallace Collection** is best known for the old master paintings, French 18th century works of art and the collection of arms and armour. The Italian paintings include works by Titian, Canaletto and Guardi. Here also are Rembrandt's *Titus*, Hal's *The Laughing Cavalier*, Poussin's *Dance to the Music of Time* and Velazquez's *Lady With a Fan*. English paintings include works by Reynolds, Gainsborough and Lawrence. 18th century French art is represented by the paintings of Watteau, Boucher and Fragonard and furniture by the boulle marquetry of brass and tortoiseshell and veneers of exotic woods, including the chest of drawers made for Louis XV's bedroom at Versailles. There is a large collection of Sevres porcelain and fine examples of gilt-bronzes, clocks and

gold snuff boxes. The arms and armour fill four galleries –
three contain European pieces and the fourth an oriental
collection.

Special events
For details of future exhibitions, phone Wallace Collection.

Shop
Shop open during museum hours sells catalogues, picture
books, guides, slides, prints, postcards and greetings cards.

Disabled
A wheelchair and a lift providing access to the first floor are
both available on request.

WALTHAMSTOW MUSEUM
(See Vestry House Museum.)

WAR ROOMS
(See Cabinet War Rooms.)

WELL HALL
(See Tudor Barn AA Gallery.)

WELLINGTON'S HOUSE
(See Apsley House.)

WEMBLEY STADIUM
Wembley, Middlesex HA9 0DW
Tel: 01-903 4864
Underground: Wembley Park

Open
Daily. Tours at 10, 11 a.m., 12 noon, 2, 3 p.m. all the year and
4 p.m. summer only.
Closed Thurs and day before, during and after an event,
Christmas Day, Boxing Day and New Year's Day.

Admission charges
Children £1.
Adults £1.50.
OAP £1.
Parties
over 20 get 10% discount.

The Guided Tour of **Wembley Stadium** offers a
comprehensive view of the stadium. Visitors have the
opportunity to see the players' changing rooms – kitted out for
match day; climb the famous steps to receive the cup and relax
in the Royal Box and Retiring Rooms. On display is the
famous Wembley Trophy Cabinet with its cups and medals
dating back 50 years, and of course the hallowed turf. A new
audio-visual presentation enables visitors to relive all the great
moments from the past including the 1924 Empire Exhibition,
the 1948 Olympic Games and England's World Cup triumph
in 1966 plus many other events that have made history at
Wembley over 60 years.

Educational provision
For educational groups, projects, competitions and
questionnaires can be provided on application.

Refreshments
A free soft drink is included with the tour.

Shop
Shop open 9.30 a.m. – 5.30 p.m. sells souvenirs of Wembley
and top football teams.

Disabled
Special facilities can be made available for the disabled and
those arranging an organised visit should inform the stadium
three weeks in advance. It should be noted, however, that as

there are many steps at the Stadium, these could be inconvenient for elderly or handicapped people.

WESLEY'S HOUSE AND THE MUSEUM OF METHODISM

47 & 49 City Road, London EC1Y 1AU
Tel: 01-253 2262

Underground: Moorgate and Old Street

Open
10 a.m. – 4 p.m. Mon to Sat.
Closed on Sun, except for a Historical walkabout at about 12.15 p.m. which includes, free of charge, the House.

Admission charges
50p per person for each museum.
Educational parties by arrangement.

Wesley's House – his London home from 1779 to 1791 – contains many letters, documents, John Wesley's personal effects and furniture, and several portraits. The Prayer Room is furnished simply with his chair, table and kneeler and here he began each day at 4 a.m. The Museum Room contains personal belongings including the electrical machine which was used in the treatment of many who came to his clinics.

The Museum of Methodism, in the Chapel Crypt, has historical objects, pictures, educational wall charts, posters and photos illustrating the world-wide growth of Methodism. In a small enclosed lecture theatre, videos and slides can be shown. Curators are always on duty and very willing to talk about the exhibits.

Educational provision
A brief guide to Wesley's House is available free, and also a children's guide. Lectures are occasionally given, for example, to 'A' Level students.

Refreshments
A vending machine sells drinks and picnic lunches can be
eaten in the garden of the House.

Shop
Shops at the House and the Museum are open from 10 a.m. –
4 p.m. selling souvenirs and books on Wesley.

WESTMINSTER ABBEY

**Chapter Office, 20 Dean's Yard, London SW1P 3PA
Tel: 01-222 5152**

Underground: Westminster

Open
The Nave and Cloister   8 a.m. –6 p.m. Mon, Tues, Thurs to
Sat; 8 a.m. – 7.45 p.m. Wed; Sun between Services but guiding
not permitted on Sun.
Royal Chapels, Poets' Corner and Statesmen's Aisle   9 a.m. –
4.45 p.m. (last admission 4 p.m.) Mon to Fri; 9 a.m. – 2.45
p.m., 3.45 – 5.45 p.m. (last admission 5 p.m.) Sat.
College Garden   Apr – Sept 10 a.m. – 6 p.m. Thurs only;
Oct – Mar 10 a.m. – 4 p.m. Thurs only.
Chapter House   Mar 15 – Oct 15 9.30 a.m. – 6.30 p.m.
Oct 16 – Mar 14 10.30 a.m. – 4 p.m. Weekdays.
Chapter Library   May – Sept 12 noon – 3 p.m. Wed.
Exhibition of Abbey Treasures   10.30 a.m. – 4.30 p.m.
(last admission 4 p.m.) Daily.
The Abbey is never closed.

Admission charges
The Nave and Cloister, College Garden and Chapter Library
Free.
Royal Chapels, Poets' Corner and Statesmen's Aisle
Children   (under 16)   70p.
Adults   £1.40.
OAP and Students   70p.

School Parties
Children 35p.
Adults 70p.
Chapter House
Children 25p.
Adults 50p.
OAP 25p.
Exhibition of Abbey Treasures
Children 20p.
Adults 40p.
OAP 20p.
Supertours conducted by Vergers include comprehensive visits to the Abbey, the Royal Chapels, the precincts, the 900 years old College Garden, and, if available, the famous Jerusalem Chamber.
Tours last about an hour and a half and bookings should be made at the Inquiry Desk or by phone (tel: 01-222 7110).
Tours commence *Apr – Oct* 10, 10.30, 11 a.m., 2, 2.30, 3 p.m. Mon to Fri; 10, 11 a.m., 12.30 p.m. Sun; *Nov – Mar* 10, 11 a.m., 2, 3 p.m. Mon to Fri; 10, 11 a.m., 12.30 p.m. Sat.
Charge for Supertour is £3.50 including all entrance charges.

Westminster Abbey is an architectural masterpiece of the 13th-16th centuries, presenting a unique pageant of British history – the Confessor's Shrine, the tombs of Kings and Queens, and countless memorials to the famous and the great. It has been the setting for every Coronation since 1066 and for numerous other royal occasions.

Today it is still a church dedicated to regular worship and to the celebration of great events in the life of the nation. Literary men are commemorated in Poets' Corner, a tradition beginning with Chaucer and continuing through Spenser, Milton, Shakespeare, Dr Johnson, Wordsworth, Keats and most recently Byron and Dylan Thomas among others.

Brass rubbing can be done in the North Cloister Mon to Sat from 9 a.m. – 5.30 p.m. (tel: 01-222 2085).

Educational provision
An extensive teachers' pack is available and a work booklet.

An experienced school-teacher guide is available, free of charge, to meet every school party, and can be called upon to do as much or as little guiding and explanation as desired.

Refreshments
For a 6 week season in high summer, meals and light refreshments are served in the College Hall, normally used as the dining room of Westminster School. At other times, cups of coffee can be purchased at the North Cloister.

Shop
Bookshop open weekdays April to October 9.30 a.m. – 5 p.m. and November to March 9.45 a.m. – 5 p.m. sells a wide range of books, films and souvenirs.

Disabled
There is access to Nave and Cloisters, Ambulatory and Transept but not to Henry VII Chapel or Shrine.

WESTMINSTER CATHEDRAL

Ashley Place, London SW1 (Correspondence to Cathedral Clergy House, 42 Francis Street, London SW1P 1QW)
Tel: 01-834 7452

Underground: Victoria
British Rail: Victoria

Open
7 a.m. – 8 p.m. Daily.
Never closed.

Admission charges
Free.

Westminster Cathedral is a Roman Catholic Cathedral built in 1895-1903 in early Christian Byzantine style. Marbles from 100 countries are found in floors, pier facings and pillars and

the Blessed Sacrament Chapel has mosaics by Boris Anrep.
Statues include a bronze of St Theresa of Lisieux by Manzu
and a 15th century alabaster statue of Our Lady and Child. The
Stations of the Cross are by Eric Gill. The crypt contains the
bodies of Cardinal Wiseman, first Archbishop of Westminster
and his successor, Cardinal Manning. Here are also the tombs
of Cardinals Griffin and Godfrey.

Educational provision
Guided tours are available by arrangement only
(tel: 01-828 5116).

Shop
Gift shop open 10 a.m. – 5 p.m. daily and bookshop open
10 a.m. – 5 p.m. Mon to Fri, half day Saturday.

Disabled
Ramp on the South Side of the building allows access.

WHIPSNADE PARK ZOO

Whipsnade, near Dunstable, Beds LU6 2LF
Tel: (Whipsnade) 0582 872171

British Rail: Luton

Open
10 a.m. – 6 p.m. (or dusk whichever is earlier) Daily.
Closed Christmas Day.

Admission charges
Children (5 – 16) £1.30, under 5 free.
Adults £2.65.
OAP £1.
Party rates (20 and over)
Children £1.15
Adults £2.30
Same for handicapped visitors in parties of 6 and over.

Whipsnade Park Zoo is an original open zoo and a conservation centre for some of the world's wildlife. In lovely country at the edge of the Chilterns, dolphins play and herds of wild animals graze in peace. Many – like Whipsnade's famous White Rhinos – are scarce in the wild. Some, such as the Przewalski's Wild Horse, may be extinct outside captivity.

The Zoo has its own special train service which runs through the paddocks close to the animals. This runs on fine afternoons between Easter and September from midday to an hour before closing time. In winter the train runs at weekends and sometimes in the school holidays.

Educational provision
Worksheets are available and lecture tours for school parties are given every weekday from the end of April to mid-July, except for May Day and the Spring Bank holiday week. Contact the Education Officer at London Zoo.

Refreshments
Cafeteria open during Zoo hours and kiosks in the summer season.

Shop
Shop open from 10 a.m. until a quarter of an hour before closing sells films and souvenirs.

Disabled
Toilets, and wheelchairs can be hired.

WHITBREAD HOP FARM

Beltring, Paddock Wood, Kent TN12 6OG
Tel: 0622 872068 and 0622 872408

British Rail: Beltring and Paddock Wood

Open
Apr 2 – Oct 27   10 a.m. – 5.30 p.m. Tues to Sun.
Closed Nov – Mar and Mon.

Admission charges
Children 75p.
Adults £1.50.

This award-winning working **Hop Farm** is situated in the heart of one of the most beautiful and historic parts of England. Over 1,000 acres, it has the world's largest group of Victorian Oasts and these form a fascinating group with the long galleried barns. During the hop-picking season, visitors can enter the oast houses and watch the hops drying on the special floor and see the hand-operated hop presses. The Hop Farm retains many traditional methods and the many changes in production can be seen by wandering among the barns. In one barn is an ever-growing collection of old carts, hop-picking machines, cultivators, and other implements. In another, are old tools and implements once commonplace to the blacksmith, wheelwright or the farmer's wife. The Farm is also the home of the famous retired, young and holidaying Whitbread Shire Horses. In one of the oldest oast houses is a working craft centre with demonstrations from weavers, potters, and other craftspeople.

Visitors can follow the nature trail across fields, hedges and woodlands where wildlife abounds, the woodpecker, kingfisher and heron in particular making their home in the wooded banks of the River Medway.

Special events
For details of future events, phone the Farm.

Educational provision
A variety of worksheets are available and a half-hour video on *Hopping in Kent* – made by Tyne Television – shows continuously. The museum won the 1983 Times and RICS Conservation Award in the Education Class. A courier takes education groups on a 1–1½ hour tour.

Refreshments
Tea room open 10 a.m. – 5.30 p.m.

Shop
Shop open 10 a.m. – 5.30 p.m. selling souvenirs.

Disabled
Ramps for the disabled provide access to farm areas, and there
are special toilets. Certain areas of the museum are
inaccessible.

WHITECHAPEL ART GALLERY

80 Whitechapel High Street, London E1 7QX
Tel: 01 377 0107

Underground: Aldgate East

Open:
11 a.m.–6 p.m. Tues to Sun

Admission charges:
Occasional charges for exhibitions but usually free and
pre-booked groups free

The **Whitechapel Art Gallery** usually mounts temporary
exhibitions for about six weeks. Visitors should phone the
gallery for its current details.

Educational provision
A lecture room, education room and audio-visual room are
available.
There are also teachers' information sheets, exhibition sheets,
and guided tours and workshops can be arranged.

Refreshments
A cafeteria is open during gallery hours selling a wide range of
home-cooked food, including vegetarian dishes.

Shop
Shop open during gallery hours. Sells art books, magazines,
posters, postcards and art materials.

Disabled
Access is possible to all public parts of the buildings. There are
special toilets, and sound enhancement in the lecture theatre.

WHITEHALL

1 Malden Road, Cheam, Sutton, Surrey
Tel: 01-643 1236

British Rail: Cheam

Open

Oct – Mar   2 – 5.30 p.m. Wed, Thurs and Sun;
10 a.m. – 5.30 p.m. Sat.
Apr – Sept   2 – 5.30 p.m. Tues to Fri, Sun and Bank holiday
Mon; 10 a.m. – 5.30 p.m. Sat.
Closed Mon, Tues and Fri from Oct to Mar.

Admission charges

Children   25p.
Adults   50p.
School Parties
By appointment, usually in the mornings.

Whitehall has permanent exhibitions of material from the
Nonsuch Palace, built in the time of Henry VIII and destroyed
by Charles II. The House is a continuous jetty timber-framed
house built in 1500, added to in the 17th century and weather-
boarded in the 18th. The back garden has a herb garden and
newly-restored timber well-head over the original well.

Special events

For details of future events, phone Whitehall.

Educational provision

Each school party is given an individual tour of the house with
a talk by the Curator, following consultation with the class
teacher, and concentrating on topics studied e.g. Tudor
environment, building methods, etc. A guidebook is available
costing 40p.

Refreshments

Cafeteria open during visiting hours. Refreshments for schools
by arrangement.

Shop

Shop open during visiting hours sells postcards, books and
souvenirs.

WILLIAM MORRIS GALLERY

Lloyd Park, Forest Road, London E17 4PP
Tel: 01-527 5544 extension 4390

Underground: Walthamstow Central

Open
10 a.m. – 1 p.m. and 2 – 5 p.m. Tues to Sat.
Closed Sun, Mon and all Public holidays.

Admission charges
Free.

The **William Morris Gallery** is a permanent collection of
works illustrating the achievements and influence of Morris
and kept at Water House, his childhood home. William
Morris was a designer, craftsman, poet and socialist and the
displays show the development of his career from the
medievalism of early designs to the virtuoso patterns of the
1880s and 90s. Wallpapers, embroideries, furniture, rugs,
stained glass and ceramics are all represented. In some cases
drawings and finished artefacts are displayed together to show
the processes of designing and making. This collection is
complemented by displays of decorative arts and designs by
Burne-Jones, Rossetti, and the Century Guild, and paintings
and drawings by the Pre-Raphaelites and Frank Brangwyn.

Parties can arrange to have gallery talks and study sessions
(maximum number 10) tailored to meet the party's needs.
Visitors can arrange sketching lessons in the gallery or
adjoining park. There is a regular programme of exhibitions
and visitors are encouraged to phone and ask for details.

Educational provision
Project packs, slide packs, study notes and handling material
are available for educational visits. The reference library may
be used by appointment.

Shop
Sales desk open during gallery hours sells postcards,
facsimiles, information sheets and gift wrap.

WIMBLEDON LAWN TENNIS MUSEUM

All England Lawn Tennis Club, Church Road, Wimbledon, London SW19 5AE
Tel: 01-946 6131

Underground: Southfields

Open
11 a.m. – 5 p.m. Mon to Sat; 2 – 5 p.m. Sun.
Closed during the Wimbledon fortnight and the preceding Fri, Sat and Sun, except for those attending the Tournament.

Admission charges
Children   75p.
Adults   £1.50.
OAP   75p.

The **Wimbledon Lawn Tennis Museum** tells the story of Lawn Tennis from its origins to the present day. On show are equipment, photographs, costumes, jewellery, and special displays including the world-famous Gentlemen's Dressing Room of 1877.

A visit includes the opportunity to view and photograph the unique Centre Court. A feature of the visit is an audio-visual theatre showing films of famous matches.

Shop
Shop open during museum hours sells clothing, jewellery and Wimbledon souvenirs.

Disabled
There is a toilet for the disabled.

WIMBLEDON WINDMILL MUSEUM

Windmill Road, Wimbledon Common, London SW19 5NQ
Tel: 01-788 7655

Underground: Wimbledon

Open
Easter – mid-Nov   2 – 5 p.m. Sat and Sun; 2 – 5 p.m. Bank
holidays (staff permitting).
Closed Mon to Fri and mid-Nov to Easter.

Admission charges
Children   10p.
Adults   25p.
School Parties
By arrangement.

Wimbledon Common Windmill Museum is believed to be the
only remaining example of a hollow post flour mill in this
country. Charles March built the Windmill in 1817 and the
name 'hollow post' derives from the fact that the shaft driving
the machinery passes through the hollowed-out core of the
main supporting post, which differs from the normal type of
mill. Although it no longer functions as a mill, its sweeps
(sails) can still turn. The first floor is now a museum of
windmills which shows the history of windmilling in England
and displays relics of other windmills which have now
disappeared.

Refreshments
Cafeteria open during mill hours.

Shop
Sales desk selling postcards and booklets.

WINDSOR CASTLE

Windsor, Berks
Tel: (Windsor) 95 68286

British Rail: Windsor

Open
Castle Precincts
July and Aug   10 a.m. – 7.15 p.m. Daily.
Sept 1 – Oct 26   10 a.m. – 5.15 p.m. Daily.
Oct 27 to Dec 31   10 a.m. – 4.15 p.m. Daily.

State Apartments
June 29 to Oct 26 10.30 a.m. – 5 p.m. Mon to Sat;
1.30 – 5 p.m. Sun.
Oct 27 to Dec 8 10.30 a.m. – 3 p.m. Mon to Sat.
Queen Mary's Dolls' House and *Exhibition of Drawings*
June 29 to Oct 26 10.30 a.m. – 5 p.m. Mon to Sat;
1.30 – 5 p.m. Sun.
Oct 27 to Dec 21 and Dec 27–31 10.30 a.m. – 3 p.m. Mon
to Sat.
St George's Chapel
July to Oct 26 10.45 a.m. – 4 p.m. Mon to Sat; 2 – 4 p.m. Sun.
Oct 27 to Dec 31 10.45 a.m. – 3.45 p.m. Mon to Sat;
2 – 3.45 p.m. Sun.

Closed
State Apartments Dec 9 to 31 and Suns from Oct 27 to Dec 8.
Queen Mary's Dolls' House and Exhibition of Drawings
Dec 22 to 26 and Suns from Oct 27.
The Castle is always subject to closure, sometimes at very
short notice, and visitors are advised to phone to check before
arrival.

Admission charges
Castle Precincts Free.
State Apartments
Children (5-16) 60p.
Adults £1.40.
OAP 60p.
Queen Mary's Dolls' House and *Exhibition of Drawings* **Each**
Children 20p.
Adults 60p.
OAP 20p.
St George's Chapel
Children 60p.
Adults £1.30.
OAP 60p.

Windsor Castle was begun in 1070 as a motte and bailey
structure. The Royal Apartments were started in the twelfth
century and St George's Chapel in the fifteenth. The imposing

entrance gateway was built by Henry VIII. St George's Chapel is one of the finest examples of the late medieval style of English architecture known as 'Perpendicular'. The chapel has a very fresh look as its fine vaulting has had to be thoroughly restored this century. It has one of the finest collections of heraldic material – enamelled shields – in the world.

Queen Mary's Dolls' House was given to Her Majesty in 1923 and is an exquisite work of craftsmanship and a valuable record of a past generation. The books in its library include works specially written by G K Chesterton and Rudyard Kipling, while tiny paintings were contributed by Sir William Nicholson, Sir William Orpen and Sir A J Munnings.

The Exhibition of Drawings has works by Leonardo da Vinci, Holbein and other artists, chosen from the Queen's collections.

The State Apartments are open to the public when the Queen is not in official residence and consist of imposing reception and ceremonial rooms and smaller, more personal, rooms; all sumptuously furnished. The Apartments have woodcarvings by Grinling Gibbons, Gobelins tapestries, busts by Roubiliac, ceilings by Antonio Verrio, and an Aubosson carpet presented to Her Majesty by President de Gaulle in 1960.

WINDSOR SAFARI PARK

Winkfield Road, Windsor, Berkshire SL4 4AY
Tel: (Windsor) 075 35 69841

British Rail: Windsor

Open
Summer   10 a.m. – 6.30 p.m. Daily.
Winter   10 a.m. – 3.30 p.m. Daily.
Closed Christmas Day.

Admission charges

Children   (under 4 free)   £3.50.
Adults   £4.50.
OAP   £3.50.
Party Rate (20 or more people)
Children   £2.
Adults   £3.
OAP   £2.
School Parties
Children £1.50; one teacher free with every 10 children; extra teachers £2.
Various concessions are offered to organisations (send for details).

Windsor Safari Park covers over 140 acres. It has seven drive-through reserves with giraffes, zebra, camels, llamas, elephants, baboons, vultures, tigers, lions, timber wolves and cheetahs. Many animals can also be seen on foot – chimps, rhinos, monkeys, and there are several bird aviaries. The new Animal Magic exhibit has young lions, tiger cubs and small primates and a nocturnal section with kinkajou and bush babies. Main attractions are the dolphin and killer-whale shows starting at 12 noon and 3 p.m. in the winter and on the hour throughout the afternoon in the summer. Parrot shows begin at 11 a.m. and run throughout the afternoon.

Refreshments
Burger Bar and Restaurant (which must be booked for parties).

Shop
Shop open during visiting hours sells postcards, books, china and porcelain ornaments, camera film and souvenirs.

Disabled
Special toilets available and all the main areas are accessible by wheelchair.

WISLEY ROYAL HORTICULTURAL SOCIETY GARDEN

Wisley, Woking, Surrey GU23 6QB
Tel: (Guildford) 0483 224163

British Rail: West Byfleet

Open
Feb – Oct   10 a.m. – 7 p.m. (or sunset if earlier) Mon to Sat;
2 – 7 p.m. (or sunset) Sun.
Nov – Jan   10 a.m. – 4.30 p.m. Mon to Sat; 2 – 4.30 p.m. Sun.
Closed Christmas Day.

Admission charges
Children   80p.
Adults   £1.60.
Parties
£1.40 for ticket obtained in advance.
School Parties
70p each for tickets obtained in advance.

Wisley Royal Horticultural Society Garden can be described
as 'A Garden for all Seasons', worth visiting at any time of the
year, even in the depth of winter. Visitors from all over the
world come to see its 240 acres. There is a very full range of
ornamental plants grown in their appropriate setting of Rock
Garden, Borders, Formal Beds, and Glasshouses, as well as
areas devoted to the cultivation of vegetables and fruit.
Additionally, there is a large area for trials of new varieties of
flowers and vegetables. A major attraction is the series of
Small Model Gardens which were created to show what can be
done on a small scale, at various levels of expertise and making
the best use of available space.

Refreshments
Cafeteria open 10.30 a.m. – 5.30 p.m. from February to mid-
November with a large range of dishes suitable for children.

Shop
Two shops open during visiting hours selling gifts, books and
plants.

Disabled

Toilets and the greater part of the Garden is accessible to wheelchairs. There is a special garden showing ways by which gardening can be made possible, and more enjoyable, for people suffering from various physical handicaps.

ZOO WATERBUS

(See London Waterbus Company.)

Index

277